THE ROMANCE OF THE MINISTRY

The Romance of the
MINISTRY

By

RAYMOND CALKINS

THE PILGRIM PRESS

BOSTON AND CHICAGO

PRINTED IN THE UNITED STATES OF AMERICA

To the memory of my dear friend
Alexander L. McKenzie
at whose request I have written this book

"The minister's calling, to one who is fond of it, is an endless romance."—

GEORGE A. GORDON

ACKNOWLEDGMENTS

Acknowledgments are made to the following publishers for their courtesy in permitting the use of quotations from their copyrighted publications:

Houghton Mifflin Company: *Letters of Franklin K. Lane; College Life* by LeBaron Russell Briggs; *Political Essays* by James Russell Lowell; *The Quick and the Dead* by Gamaliel Bradford; *Culture and Religion* by J. C. Shairp.

Marshall Jones Company: *The Life Indeed* by John F. Genung.

Oxford University Press: *The Life of Sir William Osler* by Harvey Cushing.

Dodd, Mead and Company: *The Rough Road, Idols, The Wonderful Year, The Morals of Marcus Ordeyne, The Red Planet* by William J. Locke.

Fleming H. Revell Company: *The Romance of Preaching* by Charles Silvester Horne.

Abingdon-Cokesbury Press: *The Faith by Which the Church Lives* by Georgia Harkness; *The Pastor-Preacher* by William A. Quayle.

Atlantic Monthly: "Human or Superhuman" by Charles M. Sheldon.

Christendom: "Another Fifty Years?" by Angus Dun; "Evangelism in Our Day" by Hugh T. Kerr.

Also to Bishop William Appleton Lawrence, Charles A. Ellwood, Charles R. Zahniser, Howard J. Chidley for permission to use quotations from their writings, and to Mrs. Harry A. Garfield for the use of a quotation from an address of Doctor Garfield.

FOREWORD

WHEN, in the year 1914, C. Silvester Horne, that manly Christian, brilliant preacher, social prophet, member of Parliament, came to America to deliver the Beecher lectures at Yale, he chose for his subject "The Romance of Preaching." Preaching, he said, has a romantic past, a romantic gospel, romantic possibilities. "Preaching can never lose its place," he wrote, "so long as the mystery and wonder of the human spirit remain." It is precisely this mystery and this wonder which make up the romance of the pastoral ministry. The parish minister deals daily with men and women and children in every possible condition and circumstance of life who fascinate him because they illustrate these wonders of the human spirit. All that any minister has to do in order to transform his ministry from routine to romance, to turn its water into wine, is to fasten his attention on the human material with which he has to deal. The defect of our modern ministry is that too often the minister deals with ideas, with abstractions, with the material aspects of his task, and fails to see that the highest possibilities alike of his happiness and of his influence lie in the realm of the human spirit. If he cares for anything more than he cares for human beings he can never know the real joy and the real romance of the ministry. "The man who despises the petty feelings and frailties of mankind is doomed to remain in awful ignorance of that which is of beauty and pathos in the lives of his fellow-creatures." [1] "That the world knows little of

[1] William J. Locke in *The Rough Road*, p. 275. Dodd, Mead and Company, publishers.

its greatest men is a commonplace. With far more justice it may be stated that of its least men this world knows nothing and cares less." [2] Well, the parish minister who is above all else interested in the petty feelings and frailties of men, and cares a great deal and thus knows much of the least of men, finds himself in a romantic world. He learns that "where human beings live and love and suffer there is an eternal significance beneath the commonplace and that if we grasp it, it leads us to the root of life;" that "in every human being lies the spark of immortal beauty to be fanned into flame by one rightly directed breath;" [3] that if he but looks for it he will find the soul of goodness in every human creature. To find it, to bring it to life, is his supreme interest. He moves with increasing delight and happiness in this world of his, his parish, which is filled with human interest. Every day offers him new and unexpected opportunities of knowing people in every emergency and vicissitude of their lives. To have them come to him, to have the liberty of going to them he counts his supreme privilege. Thus his days are filled with romance, beauty, poetry. His work never grows stale. Year by year it becomes more rich, more alluring. It is only as he loses himself in this humble, unnoticed daily ministry to individuals that he discovers the deepest joys and satisfactions of his life.

It is from this point of view that these chapters are written. Only this idea can justify a new book on the

[2] *Ibid.*, p. 8.
[3] William J. Locke in *The Wonderful Year,* p. 123, and *The Red Planet,* p. 339. Dodd, Mead and Company, publishers.

pastoral office of the ministry. For some ministers, as the
years go by, the glory seems to fade. There are the inevitable difficulties, disappointments, disillusions. And
there is no tragedy in all the world like that of the disillusioned minister. He begins in high hope and courage.
But little by little he "loses the sense of the splendid possibilities of his vocation. The beauty is off the morning
sky, the glow of the dawn is past. He has

'seen it die away
And fade into the light of common day.' " [4]

But now let an angel come and wake him "as a man that
is wakened out of his sleep;" [5] let him elevate the human
side of his ministry to the place of supreme concern and
importance and he is "by the vision splendid on his way
attended," and his life never loses the glow of day. For he
has discovered the true and lasting romance of the ministry.

This is not a formal treatise on the pastoral office. Its
pages are intended to be suggestive merely, throwing some
light it may be on the motives that inspire it, the faith
that sustains it, the methods that guide it, the ends to
which it is directed. It is all written under the deep conviction that if it is faithfully performed, no work to which
a man may give himself has deeper influence or more
abiding significance.

RAYMOND CALKINS

Cambridge, Massachusetts,
September 1943

[4] C. Silvester Horne, *The Romance of Preaching*, p. 45. Fleming H.
Revell Company, publishers.
[5] *Zechariah 4:1.*

TABLE OF CONTENTS

xiii

CHAPTER 1

Let No Man Despise Thee

✠ ✠ ✠ ✠ ✠ ✠ ✠

W HEN the Apostle Paul, in writing to the Romans, exhorted them not to think of themselves more highly than they ought to think, he did not have the parish minister in mind. But when he did, as in the pastoral epistles to Timothy, he reversed the idea and bade him maintain his self-respect and cherish the sense of the significance of his calling. The danger today as then, with rare exceptions, is that the minister will take too low views of his importance and be tempted to self-disparagement.

The minister does not bulk so large in the minds of men as he once did. The day is gone when intellectually and socially he was one of the most prominent men in the community. He lacks the prestige and the authority of the position that once was his. The profession of the ministry has suffered a certain decline in popular estimation. The eclipse of faith in the midst of a world devoted to material interests has resulted in a similar obscuration of the dignity of the professional ministry. This may be illustrated by the remark of a man who, on being told that the son of a friend of his was to enter the ministry, replied: "Why does he not go in for something real?"

The average parish minister seems to occupy an insignificant position today in comparison with the educators, authors, industrialists, lawyers and statesmen, whose achievements are everywhere recognized. His seems to be a very humble rôle. His name is rarely in the papers. His sermons are neither broadcast nor published. He works year in and year out, yet no one outside the narrow confines of his own parish has the remotest knowledge of what he is doing.

The result of all of this is likely to be a certain unconscious self-depreciation upon the part of the minister. He is apt to underestimate the dignity of his calling, the importance of his work, his value to the world to which he belongs. He needs to recover a vast faith in himself and in what he is doing. He must neither despise himself nor let anyone else despise him. He must go his way with courage and with pride, convinced as he ought to be, as he has every right to be, that he is an indispensable member of the community of which he seems to be such an insignificant member.[1] He must think of himself as highly as he ought to think.

When Jesus explained to his disciples what their rôle and mission in life was to be, he did not promise them exalted positions in which they were to be seen and heard of men. On the contrary, he used very simple and homely figures of speech to describe their careers. They were not to stand on any eminence. Indeed they were to be inconspicuous and unnoticed. Yet their influence was to be profound, far-reaching and pervading. They were to be candles to illumine darkness. They were to be bits of

[1] "Who should be proud of their calling if not we? What other history has equalled our own? Think of the procession of the preachers — was ever such romance? Was ever love exalted to so pure a passion? They kept the soul of humanity alive. Let every preacher in no matter how small a parish who preaches to no matter how meager a congregation remember to what a majestic fraternity he belongs and what romantic traditions he inherits." — C. Silvester Horne, *The Romance of Preaching*, pp. 46, 47. Fleming H. Revell Company, publishers.

3

leaven to stir up and cause to effervesce a life that otherwise would be stale and static. They were to be the salt of the earth.

Now salt is the humblest of products. It disappears absolutely from sight. No one notices it except it be absent. Yet how indispensable it is. It gives flavor and zest to what otherwise would be unpalatable, and by its antiseptic qualities it prevents putrefaction. The world could not do without it.

Just so, Jesus reminds his disciples, his appointed ministers, it is possible that yours is to be a life of obscurity, that you will have no pride of appearance or position or outward recognition. Yet at the same time, yours may be a life of the utmost significance and of fundamental importance and influence. When we turn the page from the Gospels to the Book of the Acts, nine out of the twelve apostles completely disappear from view and the names of the other three do not linger beyond the middle of the book. But these men did not disappear off the face of the earth; they disappeared under it. And their apostolic living was the regenerating influence that re-created the world.

So today obscurity does not connote insignificance. Because one is inconspicuous, it does not follow that he is without influence. The essential romance of the ministry today lies precisely here: that without the outward sanctions that ennobled it in days that are gone, it still possesses immense and fundamental importance because of the indispensable quality of life that is inherent in it which supplies the quickening influence indispensable to

4

the whole on-going life of the world. One recalls the reply of the boy who, asked what salt is, said: "Salt is what makes things taste bad if there isn't any in it." Take out of this world just as it is, leaving all others operating just as they are, the lives of its consecrated parish ministers, and before long it would be without the savor it now possesses.

If history proves anything, it proves that religion is necessary for the preservation of human society. This is the opinion of statesmen, publicists, historians, sociologists. "We have no record of a civilization which long endured which did not have a religious setting for its mores: nor of one which long endured after this setting was removed. . . . The death of religion would mean the death of higher civilization." [2] At bottom, it has come to be perceived, our problem is not an economic problem, nor a social problem, nor a political problem, but a spiritual problem. Our society, we have come to understand, is never going to be saved except by the moralization, by the spiritualization of its members. We shall never make the Golden Age out of leaden men and women. Only a new type of man can be trusted to operate our complicated and highly-geared industrial machine. The safety of the world is in the hands of the driver. And only the Man of Galilee knows the secret of making men whose hands will be steady. From this point of view, the humblest parish minister who day in and day out is teaching and seeking to put into the hearts of men the law of the Ten

[2] Charles A. Ellwood, *Reconstruction of Religion*, pp. 61, 67. The Macmillan Company, publishers.

5

Commandments and the higher law of Christ is doing a work which is essential to our social salvation.

Similarly, his work underlies that of the educationalist. That the training of the mind in intellectual processes, the sharpening of mental acumen, the acquiring of knowledge of the universe and its laws — that these alone are not sufficient is recognized by our best educational leaders. They agree that unless all of this is guided and informed by moral purpose, education of itself will land us short of nowhere. Indeed it is true that a person who is educated mentally but is without morals is more of a menace to the community than if he had not been educated at all. "The best that education can do," Dean L. B. R. Briggs of Harvard College once said, "is to make moral character efficient through mental discipline." [3] The implication of this statement is that moral character without efficiency is preferable to efficiency without morals. This idea was expressed by Dr. Richard C. Cabot, who once remarked that if he had to choose between the Church and the College, he would choose the Church. And similarly President Garfield of Williams College declared: "We believe that the trained mind becomes a danger and a menace unless it is guided, inspired, and held to a high character of work by that which the Church seeks to contribute to us all." [4]

The parish minister may lack the prominence and distinction of our great educators. He may not be decorated

[3] *College Life* by Le Baron R. Briggs, p. 91. Houghton Mifflin Company, publishers.

[4] *One Hundred and Fiftieth Anniversary Volume of the First Church of Christ in Pittsfield, Massachusetts*, p. 67.

with academic degrees or be a member of learned societies. But he should go about with a deep sense of the importance of his calling which entitles him to a high position in any community. For he is seeking to create and is creating a generation of youth who know the meaning of morals and possess within themselves the secret of moral control, conduct, and action. He is doing quietly and without outward recognition a work that is positively fundamental to human welfare.

As with society as a whole, so with individuals who are struggling to meet and rise superior to the difficulties inherent in our human existence. In his "psychograph" of Theodore Roosevelt, Gamaliel Bradford speaks of Roosevelt's "forced optimism, forcing enjoyment with the desperate instinctive appreciation that if he let the pretense drop for a moment, the whole scheme of things would vanish away. This sense of unreality is admirably suggested in Mr. Wister's comment: 'The wistfulness blurred his eyes — that misty perplexity which Sargent has caught so well.' — Bishop's life of Roosevelt ends with a quotation which seems to sum up the whole story: 'It is idle to complain or to rail at the inevitable: serene and high of heart we must face our fate and go down into the darkness.' " [5] Perhaps the function of religion in a man's life cannot be better described than to say that it removes the "misty perplexity" from one's eyes and enables one "serene and high of heart" to move on into the eternal Light. In a word, it gives one a sense of per-

[5] *The Quick and the Dead,* pp. 29, 30. Houghton Mifflin Company, publishers.

manence and reality in the midst of the mysteries of existence. Personality is lent a certain inwardness which enables it to cope with the vicissitudes of experience as it finds its center and its rest in God.

The service which the average parish minister is rendering in bringing religious re-enforcement into human lives and thus endowing them with health, sanity, poise, courage, and peace is beyond all computation. He is the ally of the physician and the psychologist and supplies what both of them recognize as indispensable to human happiness. He puts within human hearts a central inspiration which both illumines and controls their lives and destinies. He performs, quietly and unobtrusively, a fundamental task.

Thus ministers should have a sense of their dignity and worth in the world. And this should lend them a supreme confidence and an inward pride. They can afford to be without the prominence which others possess because they have this keen realization of the influence which is really theirs. Of this they have abundant testimony in the letters written them by those whom they have helped, comforted, and blessed. If these were ever published they would present an authentic and convincing apologia of the ministry to the minds of the most skeptical.[6]

Occasionally one finds a frank appreciation in the secular press of the value of the work which humble parish ministers are performing. Thus an editorial in the *Boston Herald* once spoke of:

[6] See "The Dominie Balances His Ledger," author anonymous. *Scribner's Magazine*, December 1928.

8

"this band of men, unrecognized, underpaid, over-worked, un-assuming, that never complain, never strike, who are accomplishing under conditions that make their performance little less than heroic a work that is indispensable to the stability and permanence of our civilization."

Parish ministers should move about their communities with their heads in the air, sustained and supported by the knowledge that what they are doing is of the utmost consequence for the individual and for society; that it underlies finance, banking, commerce, law, medicine, and is the spiritual foundation on which the whole edifice of society and the welfare of the individual finally rest. Foundation builders may be invisible, but their work is fundamental.

It should be a matter of pride also to the parish minister that his work is as delicate, as difficult, as arduous, as precarious as it is. One of the chief attractions of the ministry is that this is so. It makes its appeal to all that is heroic in a man. The chief of the fire department in New York City once said that when a man joined that department his act of bravery had already been achieved. All that came afterwards was simply a part of the day's work. Under present conditions it may be said that the ministry is for brave men only. If a man enters this profession with the idea that he will have an easy or a comfortable time in life, he will be swiftly disillusioned. Candidates for the ministry must choose it not in spite of its difficulties, but because of them. He must respond to Paul's gallant summons to young Timothy: "Come on and take your share of [the pastor's inevitable] hardship as a good soldier of Jesus Christ." [7] Therein lies the appeal of the ministry.

It is the most precarious of the professions. The minister is essentially an itinerant. He must be prepared at any time to move on. He cannot build his home and settle down for life like other men. Any one of a number of circumstances, or a combination of them, over which he has no control may make it wise or necessary for him to change his post. He never knows when he may have reached the limit of his usefulness in a given parish. Again, there are inflexible age-limits set in the profession. Young men are in demand. Let a minister, no matter how able or well-equipped, pass the age of fifty when men in other professions are at the zenith of their power and influence, and already he finds himself in the back waters. If already he is settled in a good parish, he may, by dint of fine intellectual and spiritual performance, maintain himself there and do his best work for many subsequent years. But he will find it increasingly difficult to secure a new parish. For with singular perversity most churches continue to look for younger men.

Again, the salary of the average minister is barely adequate to enable him to live day by day in a manner suitable to his position. How then is he able to educate his children and lay aside enough to care for his old age? The ministry is the most underpaid of the professions. A new conscience in the Church is providing pensions for the clergy. Yet these at best afford but a slender income. Ministers may

[7] *II Timothy 2:3*. R. V. (margin.)

not take the vow of poverty, but it is theirs as much as if
they did.

The ministry is the most delicate of the professions. In
a sense, it is an anomaly. The minister is God's spokesman. He utters the message that God has given him to
utter. Yet he is paid by the men into whose ears he utters it. And it is quite possible that what he says may have
the same effect upon them that Paul's preaching had upon
Demetrius and the silversmiths at Ephesus who protested:
"Ye know that by this craft we have our wealth." [8] Thus
the minister may find himself involved in the same difficulties which beset the Apostle. He does not and cannot
know how long his position may be tenable. Wise laymen
give their preachers all possible latitude. Wise preachers
avoid mental and moral conceit. For while men may
pardon vanity as a foible, they cannot forgive an over-
weening sense of moral superiority. Yet within these limits
there is always an area in which the maintenance of a
just equilibrium will be a delicate affair. This fact the
minister must face. Perhaps Edgar Guest had this in mind
when he wrote: "I have only sympathy for members of the
ministry. Theirs is the toughest job I know, bar none.
Their work is never done, I fancy, entirely to the satisfaction of members of their congregations." Or, he might
have added, to their own satisfaction.

Once more, the work of the minister is extremely arduous. It makes tremendous demands on physical and
nervous energy. He knows nothing about an eight, or a
ten, or a twelve-hour day. He is the hardest worked of

[8] *Acts 19:25*

any man in the community. Some years ago Dr. Charles M. Sheldon wrote an article for the *Atlantic Monthly* entitled "Human or Superhuman?" in which he enumerated the various tasks which the parish minister is expected to perform. He is supposed to prepare one or two sermons a week. "If the work of preaching were the only work required of the minister, it would keep him busy eight hours every day for a week." [9] He is expected to visit every family and individual in his parish, to write innumerable letters, and to act as counselor in every conceivable form of human emergency. If he gave his whole time to this, he would perform only a fraction of it. He must oversee the religious training of the youth of the church. "Such a man should have nothing else to do. Yet this is only one of the tasks out of a dozen that he is supposed to direct." For in addition he must manage the business end of the church, attend the meetings of its many organizations, "at most of which he is asked to make an address," cooperate with the musical director in the training of choirs, and discharge various civic duties. He must care for the sick and visit the stranger, conduct marriage and funeral services and respond to emergency calls. Also, he must find time for reading and for his domestic responsibilities.

In a word, he has had put upon him a superhuman task. The astonishing thing is that ministers are performing this task with a considerable degree of competency in all of its departments. The question which people who have any acquaintance whatever with his work constantly ask

[9] *The Atlantic Monthly,* January 1917.

is "How on earth does he manage to accomplish what he does?" It is a high and romantic performance. And given the requisite degree of devotion and moral fiber, the very complexity of his task, instead of deterring him from undertaking it, acts as a spur and incentive. All over the country, parish ministers are operating with courage and efficiency, with joy and a certain élan, keeping all the while above the level of their work and not being overwhelmed by it. Is not the one capable of such an achievement entitled to respect? Should not the minister engaged in such a task have pride in his profession?

Surveying from beginning to end the importance, the precariousness, the delicacy, and the difficulty of the work of the ministry, is not the apostolic injunction of Paul to Timothy fully justified: "Let no man despise thee?"

CHAPTER 2

Thoroughly Furnished Unto All Good Works

✠　　✠　　✠　　✠　　✠　　✠　　✠

AS Protestantism is now organized, the parish church depends largely for its dignity and influence and prosperity upon the personality, the character, and the ability of its ministry. In general it is true that what the minister is, that a given church is also. Often a church which has prospered under one man, languishes under his successor; or, equally often, a church which has shown few signs of vitality as administered by one man suddenly blooms into life when another takes his place. In this respect our so-called free churches suffer in comparison with the authoritarian churches whose strength lies in the institution of the Church itself, in its immutable dogmas and sacraments. The authority and influence of a church does not vary according to the personality or even the ability of the pastor. For he is but the medium through whom the grace of God is passed on to the believer. The authority and the dignity of the Church resides in the "grace," and this is not modified in any way by the personality of him through whom it passes. There can be no question that Protestantism in our modern world would be made far more stable and secure by regaining the conception of the Church as a divine organism, having a divine authority in its truth, its worship and its sacraments, and thus less dependent upon the personality and capacity of its ministers.

As it is, however, a heavy load of responsibility rests upon the shoulders of the parish minister in our Protestant churches. He must say to himself: What I am, what

I do, how I perform my work will determine to large degree the influence and prosperity of the church which is in my keeping. This fact, of itself, of course lends a certain dignity to his work. While it imposes a great responsibility, it offers also a glowing opportunity. A great appeal is made to the imagination, to one's will and ambition. It kindles the fires of a deep consecration, of a determined purpose himself to be all that an anointed minister of Jesus Christ can and ought to be in order that through him the Church shall exert its full influence upon the lives of men and thus upon the world. No more glorious possibility of human service is offered to any man than is put into the hands of the humblest parish minister in our modern world.

To know the full joy and romance of the ministry, it is above all necessary that one should have had a distinct and authentic "call" to this prophetic and priestly office. There are other ways of serving God. But the ministry is something distinct, apart, peculiar. One does not choose it; rather one is chosen for it. The hand of the Lord, in a real sense, is laid on one, and he is aware of a divine summons to his task. Thus one does not run over in his mind the possible professions that are open before him and for purely prudential reasons select the ministry as on the whole most suited to his tastes and capacities. He must repeat in his own experience what was the experience of Amos, of Isaiah, of Jeremiah, of Paul, what has always been the experience of every true prophet of God. These men did not choose their mission. They were called to it. There was a day, an hour, a time when the word of the

Lord came to them. All of this may sound very mystical, yet it is intensely real. And every true ministry is founded on the fact and reality of it. No man should ever enter the ministry who can possibly keep out of it. He must be able to say: "To this end was I born."

This deep conviction that he has been called of God to serve him in this one way will furnish the minister with the passion, the idealism, the freedom which will be the secret of his joy and of his unending enthusiasm; and it will throw the mantle of high romance over all of his work. Only this will save him from discouragement, from disillusionment and despair, and supply him with a deep and inexhaustible well of contentment as the years go by. For he will have his troubles. They will be many and various. Only he who works for spiritual ends in human lives and in human society knows the deepest agonies of the soul. Outwardly all may go well. External circumstance may spell success and prosperity. But there lie the deeper disappointments of the spiritual dreams which do not come true; the seed which does not spring to life; the delays in the realization in human society of the divine ideals. Here lies the tragedy in the experience of every true minister of Jesus Christ. What now shall save him from discouragement? What shall keep him on his feet? What shall be the inner inspiration which shall never rob him of his optimism, of his hope, of his confidence?

Nothing else, nothing less than that God has called him to his task and the conviction that whom God has called, he will never desert; that he is a laborer together with God, whose purpose can never fail. He will accept hardship, difficulty, disappointment as belonging to his lot. But these can never quench the fires of his hopes and passions. To him, it is a life of the highest adventure. At the end of his life and work, he will be more alive than he was at the beginning of it. In retrospect, he will be able to say: "I have not really known one unhappy day in all my ministry." For the happiness which has been his has underlain every temporary setback and disappointment. It has been the supreme happiness of him who has been called into this life of utmost sacrifice and service.

Two reassurances come at once to the support of one who thus enters by divine summons upon the work of the ministry. The first is that the fundamental qualities needed for the performance of his task are not those of the exceptional man. They are within the reach of every consecrated man. It is not required that he should be a man of unusual intellectual ability, that he should have outstanding traits that at once command attention and compel admiration, or that he should be gifted in any special fashion. What is demanded is virtue that is inherent in manhood as such, all touched and quickened and sweetened by the spirit of Jesus Christ. The spiritualization of average capacities rather than the possession of unusual powers is the needful element.

The second ground for hope is that ordinary abilities, when touched by the spirit of God, become extraordinary. The disciples were not ready and furnished for their apostolic work until they had had their pentecostal experience. Then see what manner of men they became! And today let a minister with no special gifts of mind or character be baptized as by fire with the Holy Spirit, and his life is given unimagined influence over the lives of other men. Nothing on earth is more romantic than the unsuspected powers thus released in the lives of God's servants who may have seemed both to themselves and to others to have only moderate human ability. Whom God chooses to be his prophet he equips for the task.

To do effective work in the ministry it is necessary that a man possess an abundance of physical and nervous health and energy. There are exceptions to this rule, but they are exceptions. It does not follow from this that a man should be deterred from undertaking this work if he knows that he is called to it, because he is not robust. The chances are that his strength will increasingly measure up to the demands that are made on it. Nothing in life is more striking than the gradual accommodation of one's powers to a task to which one's whole nature is adapted. The inward contentment and satisfaction which one experiences in performing it seem to develop the necessary physical equipment for its achievement. At the same time, it remains true that the care of his health remains for the minister one of his most sacred tasks. As a rule, ministers are long-lived in spite of the tremendous demands made upon their physical and nervous energies. This is because they live simple, austere, abstemious, if not ascetic, lives. Also they are delivered because of their spiritual resources from the fears, anxieties, and complexes which beset many people. Neither do they find themselves involved in the difficulties which cause many to collapse.

While they have heavy human burdens to bear, they live apart from that abnormal type of human existence which resembles the macabre, the frivolous, the insane.

Yet within his own sheltered sphere the minister may be tempted to excesses of effort, unwise expenditure of strength, the ignoring of the demands of nature for relaxation and recreation which are essential to physical well-being. And except he be in fine physical vigor, he is not "thoroughly furnished unto all good works." Sermons delivered in a minor key are not edifying. If a minister does not sleep well or if he is dyspeptic, he is not likely to lift up his voice like a trumpet. His impact on others will lack spontaneity, directness, freshness, elasticity. Without the humor which is the child of health, he will move with lagging gait. It was said of Henry Martyn that he had not a torpid nerve in him. That ought to be said of every parish minister. Like Sidney Lanier, he should walk habitually "beneath a broad, blue heaven of width and delight." His step should have a spring to it; his voice sound clear and bright; his very presence should be life-giving, the transmission to others of the abounding life and strength that is his. His power should be like Whitefield's: "He was something that burned men like fire, that bent them like wind, that drove them like a sea wave. You could not hit on the secret. He had it, that was all. Partly it lay in voice; but voice is a part of this personal equation. He was magnetic, whatever that may be; for this word is a name we give to a secret. Some men tell us a thing, and we hear it: other men tell us a thing, and we feel it. There is the distinction. Some men are logical engines, calculating machines: others breathe on our souls, and they rise to meet the breath as flowers do to meet the breathing of the wind of spring." [1]

At the center and source of such a life lie inexhaustible resources of physical energy. These in turn depend upon a careful ordering of one's daily living to such an end. Each must discover for himself the regimen of diet, rest, sleep, best suited to his physical needs. To this he rigidly adheres, allowing nothing to interfere with it. What may be allowable to others may not be indulged in by him. He guards his health sacredly. There are no week ends for the parish minister. What for others are days of relaxation from work are for him the most demanding days of the week. Neither is there any day of any week when he is free from care. The legend of a minister's Monday lingers on only in the minds of those who know least about him. He labors as a rule seven days in the week month after month.

Hence the necessity of self-imposed periods of rest when he escapes from the insistent demands of telephone and door-bell and gives himself up to complete repose. If wise, he will make of his vacation a time of entire relaxation, giving himself wholly to outdoor life and emptying his mind of what usually occupies it. Thus he comes fresh and invigorated and eager to his task when he resumes it. These counsels may not fit all cases. The thing essential is that every minister be thoroughly furnished physically unto all good works.

[1] Bishop William A. Quayle, *The Pastor-Preacher*, p. 84. Abingdon-Cokesbury Press, publishers.

And also he must be mentally and intellectually well fortified. It is not required that a minister be intellectually brilliant, but it is required that he be intellectually competent. No minister today can exercise a real influence if his ideas lag behind what is being thought in our modern world. The pews of any church large and small are filled today with men and women who have been trained in modern ways of thinking. Let a minister be never so devout, never so earnest, yet making it quite evident that he is unaware of the basic ideas which govern men's thinking, and he is shorn at once of his influence over them. They may respect him personally, they may revere his piety, but they simply do not listen to what he has to say. Hence the minister needs thorough training in all of the secular disciplines. He must be familiar with the findings of science, philosophy, psychology, sociology. He does not need to be learned in any one of them. But he must be acquainted with the geography of the modern mind.

Probably no generation in human history has ever had to readjust its thinking to so many facts from so many different quarters in so short a space of time as have the men and women who are alive today. In the sphere of religion and of morals this is especially true. About all of this the minister must be informed, for he is dealing with people who have been influenced, even if they have not been positively persuaded, by ideas which run wholly counter to the traditional religious teaching. Let a minister make it clear by every word and accent that he is familiar with these modern trends of thought, that he knows what has been taught by men who have questioned or denied even the most elementary assumptions upon which the whole edifice of religion and morality may be said to rest; then and then only will men listen to him while he declares his own faith and exhibits it in his teaching as well as in his life. He will not argue, neither will he rationalize. But he will betray every time he speaks in public or privately his awareness of the modern religious problem and he will capture the attention and sympathy of his hearers because they can see that he knows whereof he speaks. No minister is "thoroughly furnished unto all good works" without at least this degree of intellectual competency.

Yet a purely secular culture does not suffice. It is the background but it is not of the substance. For the minister the supreme qualification is a certain quality of spiritual being which is the gift of God alone. He must in every aspect of his life and work give unmistakable evidence that he has a constantly renewing experience of God. This gives a certain distinction to his character and performance. He gives to all who come in contact with him the subtle impression that he is a truly consecrated man, delicately sensitive to every breath of God.

In final analysis, it is the spirituality of the minister which gives him authority and wins for him the respect, the affection, the confidence of others. This immediate consciousness of God through the indwelling spirit of Jesus Christ is the innermost secret of every true ministry. Without it, his work is that of the mechanic but not of the spiritual artist. With it, what may seem to be but broken fragments of power and inspiration will be able to feed the spiritual hunger of many souls. Let any man be truly devoted to his calling as a minister of Jesus Christ, let him look for, expect, and cultivate a deepening experience of God, and there are no visible limits to his usefulness and influence.

This is the source of all true prophetic inspiration which can neither be analyzed nor defined. What is spiritual quality? "Let us call it the grasp of a Life, the knowledge of which is revealed to some babes and denied to some learned; which comes more from conduct than by study and more by the grace of God than by either. Able men lacking it or losing this quality cease to be able or to inspire leadership: and simpler, unnoticed men possessing it are literally the salt of the earth."

CHAPTER 3

Clean Hands, Righteous Lips, and a Pure Heart

✚ ✚ ✚ ✚ ✚ ✚ ✚

E VERY man's power," Phillips Brooks has said, "is measured by his task multiplied by and projected through his personality." Thus the reach and influence of our ministry will depend not only on the kind of work we are doing, but also upon the kind of men we are. We think as a rule a great deal about the first of these, but not so often of the other. Some men only have to be in order to be loved. They insensibly attract people, impress them, win their confidence. There is that about them "which defies analysis, which eludes definition, but which is found in those rare characters who gain our admiration and kindle our affection." These acquire influence not so much by what they do as by what they are.

Important in every sphere of life, the possession of such a personality in the ministry is well-nigh essential. For the parish minister's true success and real value depend directly upon his ability thus to impress the lives of those with whom he has to deal. Such is the romantic element in the work of the ministry. Its effect cannot be measured by outward and visible standards of performance. It depends for its lasting influence upon those subtle and indefinable characteristics which go to make up what we vaguely call a spiritual personality. "The gospel," it has well been said, "is not a gospel until it is told by one who is living it. It becomes true only in the mouth of one who has made it true." Always and everywhere it is the man that one is that leaves the deepest impression. Thus at a Yale commencement years ago, Justice Brewer said of President

Woolsey: "He was the grandest man that ever touched my life"; and of President Porter: "His head may have been a syllogism but his heart was the Golden Rule: elms of Yale, grand and hale, whose arms are bending o'er us."

Thus we may be sure that men will be forming their judgments of us as Christian ministers. We may be excellent preachers, good administrators, faithful pastors, yet without this "Gideon touch" of a certain spirit which shines through and illumines all that we do, we fall short of our highest and most lasting influence. Some men in the ministry have been great performers; yet their work is soon forgotten. Others have had brief or humble ministries; yet their memory lingers and they are venerated long after they have gone. And that is because of the men they were. They had a certain "immortal and unconquerable fineness of fiber," a certain "lordly and large compass of soul." The light of God illumined their lives.

Such a personality is evidently not to be acquired by any outward means. It grows out of deep, rich soil. A beautiful soul is an essentially spiritual product. There is this gradual refinement of one's being. Insensibly it is clothed with spiritual quality as with a garment. This invests with a kind of beauty all that one is and says and does. It introduces a certain imaginative and spiritual element in his dealings with men. It gives grace and meaning to the most casual happenings of everyday life. "An aroma of high feeling not to be defined but all pervading" permeates all of one's activity. Let a parish minister be such a man and he has within him the source and secret of immeasurable influence upon the lives of other men. Thus the cultivation of his inward self becomes his most sacred task: he prays that the grace of the Lord Jesus Christ may rest upon him. For the word "grace" as it is found in the New Testament means not only the undeserved loving-kindness of God in Christ to man; it denotes also the attractiveness and beauty of the person of Jesus. It is in this sense that Jesus has been called with perfect reverence the first of gentlemen. Of his dress it is said that it was a garment "without seam, woven from the top-throughout." And how exquisite was his approach to all with whom he came in contact, how delicate his courtesy. The communication of this quality of life is not the least of the gifts of Christ to his disciples.

The first evident impression which such a person as has been here described makes upon others is that of a certain refinement in appearance and manner. He is, in a word, a gentleman. Now the term "gentleman" has never been adequately defined. Perhaps it can better be felt than analyzed. Birth and breeding are often supposed to be so essential that it has been said that three generations are required to produce a gentleman. Yet some people who have both birth and breeding are not really gentlemen at all, while others who have had neither have acquired the grace and the distinction which the term connotes.

Cleanliness, we say, is next to godliness. The word is not found in the Bible. But the truth is there. Only he who hath clean hands is to ascend into the hill of the Lord. If one cannot aspire to holiness who is not morally clean, neither can one attain high levels of respect who is not physically immaculate also. Here is the little touch of what is sometimes regarded as superfluous which is an elemental necessity in the lives of all who are brought into intimate contact with other people. Hence, the parish minister cannot be too meticulously careful about his appearance. A young woman once gave up a lucrative position as secretary to a well-known university professor. When asked why she did so, she replied with deep disgust, to paraphrase her actual words, that he evidently did not know the meaning of the word "manicure." Carelessness in such matters by a parish minister is nothing short of a fatality.

Similarly, with respect to his dress. However else a minister may seek to economize, he never tries to lower his laundry bill. Ministers as a rule cannot afford expensive clothes or an elaborate wardrobe. But the clothes that they do wear can be spotless and well-pressed. Also they can be worn well. In Mrs. Wharton's well-known novel "The House of Mirth," the heroine, Lily Bart, had fallen out of her world and lived for a time with people beneath her in refinement and culture. She received a visit from an old friend. "It rested her the way he wore his clothes." It lies within the power of us all to convey the same impression of restfulness and comfort. And the effect produced goes farther than we may imagine.

Then there is what we call manner. Now manner, it has been said, makes the man. And manner, as we all know, is a different thing from manners. These can be learned from books of etiquette. But manner is a spiritual product. It involves an instinctive sense of the fitness of things. Guided by a secret intuition one infallibly does and says the thing that is right. Courtesy, it has been said, involves a complete mastery of the Golden Rule. Perhaps with even greater truth it might be added that it involves an essential reverence for the personalities of others which prevents one from acting in any way which would jar another's sensibilities. And a courtesy such as this comes only out of the deepest personal culture. Once acquired it is an immense asset in one's dealings with men.

Again, there is the matter of speech. "Be not many masters," writes James, "knowing that we shall receive the greater condemnation." [1] The words convey no meaning. Moffatt's translation gives the sense: "Do not swell the ranks of the teachers; remember, we teachers will be judged with special strictness." And then he goes on to speak about the perils of the tongue. And what he plainly meant was that if one aspired to be a teacher or a preacher, he should reckon in advance with the pitfalls into which a careless use of his tongue will cause him to stumble. Every one is bound to make mistakes at this point. But one whose position requires him to be using his tongue all of the time is in greater danger than anyone else. And a parish minister is talking constantly. He not only speaks from the pulpit. He is expected to speak on every imaginable occasion and under all kinds of circumstances. And he is talking to individuals constantly and casually. His tongue is rarely idle. From the time that he gets up till slumber seals his lips and silences his tongue, he is an inevitably voluble person. Here, says James, lies his peculiar temptation, here lurk his hidden but constant dangers. In the

[1] *James 3:1*

use which he makes of his tongue he "will be judged with special strictness."

Thus, of all men, the parish minister must accomplish the difficult task of controlling and taming the tongue. And how difficult that task is the Apostle goes on to describe. He may seem to be using extravagant language and to be employing grandiose figures of speech which may even provoke a smile. We must remember, however, that he was probably a Christian teacher himself and is describing his own difficulties, mistakes and humiliations. Try as he will, he finds the taming of his tongue an all but impossible task.

Most of us have made the same disquieting discovery. After we have arrived at varying degrees of sainthood and have succeeded in putting under foot many besetting sins, we find ourselves far from perfection in this important department of our moral being. We are inclined to agree that "if any man offend not in word, the same is a perfect man and able also to bridle the whole body." Perfection, however, is precisely what is demanded of the minister. An unwise use of the tongue which might be pardoned in another, brings him into judgment.

"Let thy speech be seasoned with salt." That is, let it be purified from all possible vulgarity. Words may be dropped carelessly that will leave an unfortunate impression, will offend by lack of good taste. Ministers cannot be too scrupulous at this point. Never will they indulge in Biblical jokes or tell anecdotes that have to do with any of the sacred offices which are theirs to perform. A minister's speech will be human, far from stilted, often light and gay; but always it will be austerely chaste. By a single semi-vulgar anecdote or reference a minister may suffer permanent loss of influence. For the idea lingers that he was capable of saying it. By contrast consider the remark of a woman who once said of her minister: "It is restful to know that never under any circumstances could he say anything that would offend the most fastidious taste."

Then, there is the danger of the irritable tongue. And there are many occasions when it has to be curbed by a consecrated will. A minister who has once lost his temper or even his equanimity has been judged with greater strictness than other men would be under the same circumstances. He must learn to hold his tongue, have the grace to give the soft answer that turneth away wrath. Composure and control must be his under the most aggravating circumstances. In season and out of season he must be capable of this high performance.

Or there is the censorious tongue. Never will the minister criticize any one of his parishioners in the presence of another. This is a ministerial crime. It may be that he will have cause for feeling that another has treated him unjustly. Yet if that person's name comes up in conversation with someone else, he will either have nothing to say about him at all, or if he says anything, it will be to that person's credit. Magnanimity and a high regard for people's virtues rather than a vivid realization of their shortcomings are the keys that unlock his lips. Gossip of any kind and all kinds is entirely outside of his world. If others indulge in it while he is present, he is invariably silent; and nothing will ever persuade him to utter any disparaging opinion about the lives or doings of others.

He will never pass unfeeling or uncharitable judgments upon those who may have made moral failures or have fallen below what was rightly expected of them. It was because of Charles Kingsley's magnificent tenderness born of deep reverence for the human soul that it was possible for his wife to write of him that "while he might smile at people's foibles he was never known to sneer at anyone." To smile at people's foibles is one thing. For if our oddities add to the world's merriment, so much the better. But to sneer is in the nature of an insult to all that is true and good in man. And of this the minister will never be guilty.

Here then is held out the possibility of high, romantic performance in a difficult sphere of life. Into this wild region Christ's spirit must enter and work the impossible. The tongue no *man* can tame. But He can tame it who when He was reviled, reviled not again. In no respect perhaps will the deep, rich native culture of the true minister of Jesus Christ more clearly show itself than in the way his speech is purged of every questionable element; his tongue is tamed and held in control in every vicissitude of daily living, and kindness, charitableness, and love become the law of his lips.

It is demanded also of the minister that his life shall be above reproach. The moral standards of the ministry are high and they are inexorable. Maltbie D. Babcock once said that a minister's life must not only be clean, it must be antiseptic. The slightest deviation from the implacable rules which govern a minister's conduct brings down upon him final condemnation. It should be a matter of pride in the profession of the ministry that this is so. In other professions it remains true that men may err in matters of personal conduct, yet if they are experts they will still be in demand and their professional standing will not be affected. The work of learned professors, successful practitioners at the bar, skilful physicians is not ended if they diverge from the accepted, conventional standards in morals. Their family life may be irregular and people may not approve, but they are not boycotted by public opinion to the degree that their pupils or clients desert them. But let a minister in even minor degree err in such matters and his career is automatically and finally ended. He must acquire and hold the reputation of an absolutely clean and incorruptible life. Even suspicion concerning it is fatal. What is lightly condoned in others is neither forgotten nor forgiven in him. Divorce is common, but a divorced minister has a hard time finding or keeping a church. Financial dealings by men prominent in the business world are sometimes questioned, yet are dismissed with a shrug. But let a minister dabble in stock speculation or be guilty of the slightest violation of financial ethics, and his usefulness as a minister is at an end. Swift and implacable judgment is visited upon him. He must avoid in every detail in life the lightest breath of scandal.

Yet temptations of every kind are in his path. His emotional life is constantly stimulated. The desire to sympathize may lead to unwise and ill-considered intimacy.

This doubtless was the cause of the tragedy in the life of Henry Ward Beecher. The president of Amherst College probably voiced the general opinion when he said that Beecher was as innocent as an unshorn lamb and equally as foolish. A prominent minister of national reputation suddenly and unaccountably disappeared from his church and from the country. He had been guilty of no crime; misconduct was never proved against him. But indiscretion there had been, and that was sufficient to terminate an eminent and useful career.

Roman Catholic priests are safeguarded to a certain extent by the fact that their conduct is governed by rigid rules prescribed by the Church. Also the clerical costume which they must always wear in public wherever they go is a certain protection. But a Protestant minister is often to all outward appearance like other men. He can go where he will and no one will ever know him to be a minister. He is governed by no outward regulations imposed by his Church. He is free to act according to his own ideas and ideals. Moreover he is expected to be "a man among men," to enter into the social life of his fellows and engage in their diversions and amusements. He can decide for himself what he considers to be wise and best in matters of personal conduct. Yet, in all of this, he is judged by the strictest standards and must never trip into error. His daily conduct must be free from anything which is not worthy of his calling. It is high romance in the sphere of personal living.

Under these circumstances, the record of the ministry as a whole is a remarkable one. A ministerial scandal of any kind is so rare that it is front-page news. The men in the ministry may be humble men. They may not possess unusual intellectual ability. But as a rule they set a high example of personal conduct; their hearts are pure and they are untouched by evil. It may be said of them, as Charles H. Spurgeon once said of William E. Gladstone: "I may not be able to believe in the infallibility of any man, but it is restful to believe in one man's integrity." People as a whole think of their ministers, and have a right to think of them, as being incapable of immoral conduct in any form. Therein lies the essential dignity of the ministry.

Clean hands, righteous lips, and a pure heart. These then are the visible characteristics of the man of God. And if, beside all of this, there is that divine inbreathing which gives him a certain spiritual distinction and wins for him the admiration and affection of those who, knowing him, instinctively trust him, then there is no way of measuring the breadth and depth of the influence that is his.

CHAPTER 4

Gird Yourselves with Humility

✠   ✠   ✠   ✠   ✠   ✠   ✠

NO part of the task of the minister often seems more prosaic, more devoid of human interest than that of parish administration. Here he has to deal with many problems of organization, of finance, of the care and use of property and many details arising from the management of parish affairs. All of this is often burdensome and vexatious, demanding much time and strength that one would be glad to devote to what seem higher, more rewarding, more spiritual employments. It is true that too many parish duties are sometimes placed upon the minister's shoulders; that he is unnecessarily and unwisely expected to care for matters that could and should be attended to by responsible laymen and women. Wise church officials seek to relieve their ministers in every possible way of the routine duties of parish management so that he can give his strength to the spiritual work to which he is specially appointed.

At the same time it is true that this whole area of the business administration of the church offers to the minister the opportunity for the exercise of high moral and spiritual qualities. For in this work the minister has to deal with men and women of varied temperaments who have ideas that may differ sharply not only from his own, but from those of their fellow-workers. These ideas and interests often compete and sometimes clash. To be in the midst of all of this; to keep unruffled, serene and courteous; to know when compromise is wise; to maintain one's patience and self-control, while at the same time guiding the affairs of the parish to certain well-defined, desirable, and never-surrendered ends — all of this is a high spiritual achievement. It calls for the exercise of certain moral virtues, the importance of which is sometimes overlooked.

Mr. Horne in his Yale lectures said that "the two endowments with which any man can go far (in the ministry) are common sense and the gift of humor." [1] Without humor, he is not likely to live happily whether or not he goes far. Rabbi Duncan declared that the qualifications for the ministry were: "Greek, Grace, Grit, Gumption." Moralists have long insisted on the importance of humor in the business of everyday living. Humor, it has been said, is the beginning and end of philosophy. Psychologists are reminding us how great a factor in the continued existence of humanity is the will to laugh. With the sense of humor we are told, "one can look mockingly upon the portentous seriousness of this ridiculous world." [2] Humor, in daily living, is what well-inflated tires are to a car. It enables one to go over the inevitable unevennesses of life without a jar or a jolt. Thus it has been affirmed that "without a sense of humor you might as well kill yourself as marry." [3]

It is even more true that without humor you might as well kill yourself as become a parish minister. Hardly a day passes in the varied activities of a busy minister's life when things and occasions do not arise which, without a

[1] Charles Silvester Horne, *The Romance of Preaching*, p. 129. Fleming H. Revell Company, publishers.

[2] William J. Locke, *Idols*, p. 15. Dodd, Mead and Company, publishers.

[3] William J. Locke, *The Morals of Marcus Ordeyne*, p. 83. Dodd, Mead and Company, publishers.

saving sense of humor, can vex and distress and depress him. Thus he becomes taut, nervous, impatient. He loses balance and control. He may even lose sleep over matters which should have been shrugged off. One wonders how much of nervous instability, even nervous exhaustion, has not been induced by the failure to see how little some things are. Many ministers take things too seriously, endow minor matters with a dignity that does not belong to them, lift them to an eminence out of all proportion to their meaning. It would make for the serenity, not to say sanity, of many a minister's mind if he could know a love that no bitterness can alienate and a gaiety of soul which can take rubs and knocks without melancholy, acrimony, or self-pity.

Oliver Wendell Holmes once said that he was deterred from entering the ministry because of the sour visages of the parsons who used to come to his father's home in Cambridge. No true minister will present any such countenance to the world. "The longer I live," wrote Franklin K. Lane, "the more I am convinced that it is our duty to be gay; not reckless, never that, not boisterous but light-hearted. . . . To be gay, one must see how very little some things are and how big other things are. And the big things are things like love and goodness and unselfishness; and the little things are the mean things . . . things that generally come out of one's vanity, one's love of one's self." [4] And, one might add, out of a distorted sense of one's personal dignity. Often this pride of self causes small vexa-

[4] *Letters of Franklin K. Lane,* p. 400. Houghton Mifflin Company, publishers.

tions to penetrate and hurt. Whereas on the one who is not thinking of himself these small matters have no effect and fall harmless from the heart that is lifted high above them.

Again, if he is to go far, a minister must have common sense. This is a homely virtue. Yet for the lack of it many a minister, able, devoted, earnest, makes grievous and sometimes fatal mistakes. He does not know when he ought to yield, to compromise, to adjust himself to other people's opinions and prejudices. He lacks perspective, patience, and tolerance. He is unable to deal with delicate situations wisely and with due regard for other people's feelings. Having made up his own mind, he can admit no other point of view. He cannot understand how opinions other than his own have any worth that demands consideration. He is impatient with dullness. It is impossible for him to make allowance for the element of doubt and uncertainty in the minds of others. He lacks resilience and the ability to accommodate and adjust his mind and conduct in harmony with conflicting points of view. The intensity of his convictions and an unyielding sense of duty prevent him from envisaging other ideas. He insists on immediate and unconditional surrender upon the part of those who disagree with him. He cannot distinguish between negligible points which may well be conceded and major principles which ought never to be abandoned. He does not know when he ought to take his stand and when he ought to yield. Thus, with the best intentions in the world, he appears to be pig-headed, short-sighted, obstinate.

Some years ago the minister of a city church was campaigning for free pews. It was a laudable ideal. The plan encountered opposition, but it was finally adopted. The action was taken, however, in the middle of the parish year when already pew-owners had paid their pew-rentals for the entire year. A prominent and devoted official of the church therefore proposed that the new plan should not go into effect until the beginning of the next fiscal year. He was actuated by conscientious motives, by a scrupulous sense of financial fair-dealing. But the minister would not yield the point. He would not brook delay. The action had been taken and must forthwith be put into effect. As a result, the official and some of his sympathizers withdrew from the church, hurt and embittered. Irretrievable damage had been done by lack of ordinary common sense. No harm would have been done by a six months' delay, and regard would have been paid to the scruples of an honest man.

By contrast, consider the action of another minister who had engaged in a similar endeavor, opposed by an outstanding church official. It was agreed that a final vote should be taken at a church board meeting on a fixed date. When the board assembled, this official was absent. It appeared that illness had prevented his attendance. Instead of taking advantage of his absence, the minister proposed that action be deferred until the next monthly meeting of the board, "because our friend has ideas on this subject which he would like us to hear." By this act of courtesy and consideration, the minister won the respect of all and eventually, without ill-feeling on the part of anyone, the proposal was accepted and put into operation.

Such a sense of the fitness of things is a spiritual gift and a spiritual achievement of a high order. "It involves a sense of proportion, a sense of relevance, judgment as to the time to speak and the time to be silent, what to say and what not to say, knowledge of what to do and what in the process of things to leave undone. In short, what we too superficially call common sense."[5] And few men have greater opportunity of being trained in this virtue than the parish minister.

Above all, he must possess the grace of humility. Only when a minister is girded with humility is he equipped for his task of dealing with men. Dante in his Purgatorio makes the purging of pride the first process to be undergone, for pride is the foundation of all sins. The purging of pride should be the minister's first task, and for the same reason. It is the source and origin of ministerial sins, shortcomings, failures. "God resisteth the proud," says the Bible. As a corollary to that it may be added: and so do men. For pride inevitably arouses the hostility of others. Human nature can stand a good deal, but it cannot stand pride in another. By a kind of subtle instinct it is stirred up to destroy it. "By pride," says a wise proverb, "cometh contention." If a man is proudful to have his own way, men silently line up against him. It is not his ideas they so much object to, as his spirit. The same ideas in a man of humbler spirit would be met, if not with approbation, at least without resistance. But pride stiffens opposition.

One may see that law at work in high places and in low;

[5] Georgia Harkness, *The Faith by Which the Church Lives,* p. 49. Abingdon-Cokesbury Press, publishers.

in matters of great moment and of little moment; in the
home, in business, in practical affairs everywhere. The
person who is most likely to have his own way is the person who is most willing not to have it. The high and
haughty man rarely gets where he wants to go. Men line
up in serried ranks against him. But watch a man of different temper and see how opposition fades and melts
away and how he arrives at his goal. Men occupy the summits of achievement and of honor in proportion as they
gird themselves with this practical and indispensable virtue
of humility. And nowhere is this more true than in the
parish, large or small. Men have strangely overlooked what
may be called the strength of humility. "All goodness
which is not humble can be seduced; all greatness which is
not purged of pride can be tripped up. But humility fears
no force, needs no outside aid, breaks the weapons of
hostility on its own breast, buries evil beneath its own
goodness, sucks the poison from hate, conquers enmity
by love and sweetness, death in victory."

We read that when the devil wanted to destroy Jesus,
he took him up "into an exceeding high mountain." And
that is where he takes the minister: a high mountain of
conceit, arrogance, ambition to have his own way. And
then destruction follows as a matter of course. On the
other hand, the minister who is girded with humility is
elevated by his fellowmen to heights of respect and honor
where he dwells secure. "Such humility is not self-abase-
ment. Rather it is . . . in fact, just what comes into life from
the elimination of the self-element. It is the projection
and intrusion of self in the foreground that puts things

46

out of proportion, conceals many things from view that are an essential part of the scene. But when self is eliminated, then for the first time life and the world are seen and treated as they really are without the glamours of self-interest and pride, without the twist of jealous prejudice or of offended selfishness to distort the view." [6] It is only the humble man who has the true perspective and thus has that attitude which is the clue to power. The one thing which the successful parish minister will avoid is pride of opinion.

James Russell Lowell once described the qualifications of a president of the United States in words which one by one may be said to describe those of the true parish minister: "by so gently guiding public sentiment that he seems to follow it; by so yielding doubtful points that he can be firm without seeming to be obstinate on essential ones; and thus gain the advantage of compromise without the weakness of concession; by so instinctively comprehending the tempers and prejudices of people as to make them gradually conscious of . . . his freedom from temper and prejudice; it is by such qualities as these that a magistrate shows himself to be a chief in a commonwealth of freemen." [7]

We are seeing in all of this what may be the romance of a parish minister's life as he learns to deal with all sorts and conditions of men in wisdom and so with a high degree of effectiveness. He moves with a kind of joy, with

[6] John F. Genung, *The Life Indeed*, p. 218. Marshall Jones Company, publishers.
[7] James Russell Lowell, *Political Essays*, Prose Works 1890, Vol. V, pp. 183, 184. Houghton Mifflin Company, publishers.

a sense of freedom and of happiness in the complex and sometimes tangled sphere of human relationships. He views the whole scene with a kind of humor and in the spirit of a broad tolerance. He refuses to become ruffled. He is courteous always, never impatient even when he meets with lack of understanding or even with injustice. He preserves always a spirit of urbanity and never loses the mastery of himself. For in him has been wrought the amalgam of two contrasted and seemingly opposite traits of character. He has both passion and patience. George Eliot has spoken of "the passionate patience of genius." The parish minister must be that kind of a genius. If he lacks passion, fails to hold before him ideals which he is resolutely determined to attain, he will be nothing but a routine performer. He will achieve nothing final, desirable, and lasting. Yet if he lacks patience he will never accomplish these high ends and at the same time preserve the peace and unity of his parish. Both virtues are indispensable and they must be fused in perfect harmony.

All of this is a wonderful school in character, and character nowhere counts for so much as in the ministry. On the occasion of the twentieth anniversary of his consecration as bishop of Massachusetts, Bishop Lawrence made an address in St. Paul's Cathedral, Boston, to the clergy of the diocese, in the course of which he used these words: "Remember when you have to deal with difficult men that you have yourselves the chance to become better men." Precisely that opportunity is offered to every parish minister. By learning the great virtues of tolerance, patience, humility, not only does he guide the affairs of his parish wisely and successfully, but he himself becomes a better man. At the conclusion of the meeting of a church board, when the discussion had disclosed sharp divergence of sentiment and the ideas of the minister had met with open opposition, a member of the board said to his minister: "You have shown me tonight what a truly Christian character is. You have never retreated or surrendered. Yet you have met other men's ideas with deference, courtesy, and control and have not insisted on having your own way. Therefore in the end you will have it and have at the same time the affection and respect of every one of us."

How true it is, therefore, that in the apparently prosaic and unimaginative sphere of parish management there is offered to the minister romantic possibilities of personal life and action.

CHAPTER 5

Are There Not Twelve Hours in the Day?

✠   ✠   ✠   ✠   ✠   ✠   ✠

ONE of the most elusive elements in experience is the element of time. Its proper management and control is one of life's most important and difficult tasks. The chronic lack of time is the common complaint of all. Time is indeed our hardest taskmaster. The greatest tyrant in the world is the timepiece. Arnold Bennett once wrote an essay entitled "How to live on twenty-fours a day." In most people's experience that is harder than to live on twenty-four dollars a week. We are constantly being overtaken by arrears of work. Indeed, it is not so true that we pursue our work as that our work pursues us. The hands of the clock sweep along behind us as an ogre, always threatening to overtake us. We are perpetually behind our schedules. "And time is conquered and our crown is won," wrote Edward Rowland Sill. And most of us would agree that anyone who has succeeded in conquering time is entitled to a crown.

Of no one's life are these reflections more true than of that of the parish minister, for he is trying to do more kinds of work at the same time than anyone else in the community. He has as many important briefs to write as any lawyer. He has as many visits to make as any doctor. He has as many committee meetings to attend as any executive. He has as many addresses to make as any public speaker. He has as much study and reading to do as any student. He has as many letters to write as many a business man. He has the same domestic cares as other people. And in addition to all of this, he is exposed to a never-ending series of demands on his time from individuals who in special emergencies need his care and attention. His work is never done. How now shall such a man budget his time so that none of these tasks shall be neglected while he keeps himself from becoming overwrought?

The problem is for him all the more serious because he can do with his time what he will. He is not obliged to fit himself into exact schedules. There is no time-clock for him to punch. He can get up when he will, go to work when he will, keep at work only as long as he will. He can do as he pleases with his twelve hours of the day. Hence he must impose upon himself, for it is not imposed on him, the ordering of his time. And upon this self-imposed mastery and use of time, the effectiveness of his ministry will depend.

He will, if he is wise, early recognize the importance of limiting the area of his activities so that he will expend the time that is his upon those duties for which he is primarily responsible. The parish minister, it must be remembered, is a specialist, and as such he must devote himself to his specialty, the care of the parish that is entrusted to his care. He will discover before he has gone far that many calls come to him for useful service, but service that is not related to what is his real business. He will be asked to serve on numerous committees, boards, and organizations. He will be invited to speak on all kinds of occasions. Somehow the impression exists that a minister is able to talk on any subject at any time. If one cannot think of anyone else to fill in, there is always the minister to fall back upon. But if he is wise, he will resist this constant outside pressure upon his time. He will not be lured by the promise of fees nor by the assurance that he is indispensable to the occasion. He will scrutinize every invitation to see if it is related to his main task and deliberately eliminate everything that lies beyond its self-imposed boundaries. These will include denominational and civic interests, for the minister must share in the broader life of the church and the community. Yet when this has been admitted there remains a host of secondary activities from which he must turn resolutely aside in order to allow a courageous concentration upon the central purpose of his life.

Again, in ordering the work of each separate day, he will learn the value of deliberate selection among the many things that he ought to do, of those things which he ought to do first and ought to do most. Though he labored twenty-four hours a day, he would never complete what really calls to be done. A minister's task is horizonless. There are no boundaries to it. Always there are more letters to be written than can be written; more calls to be made than can be made; more reading to be done than can be done; more duties to be attended to than can be attended to within the confines of a single day. Therefore there must be this quick, instant delimitation and choice of what shall be done. On running over what awaits him, he will draw a circle instantly around what shall have that day's attention and devote himself to the fine performance of that particular fragment of his total task. This he will never expect to achieve. And having surrendered the expectation of achieving it, he is never worried or harassed

54

by his uncompleted tasks. Only when this process of selection has been neglected, only when the frantic endeavor is made to compass everything that calls for attention does he suffer from a sense of frustration and defeat. No minister of even the smallest parish can keep up with the multitude of duties that legitimately make demands upon his time. That fact he faces and accepts. Having done as well as possible all that his twelve hours can hold, he leaves without despair and even without regret what has lain outside of the possibilities of that day's performance. Thus he keeps his poise, his serenity, his peace of mind and avoids the nervous tension which failure to do all that he feels he ought to do inevitably provokes. The fact is he ought not to do it all. He can never do it all. He will not try to do it all. He will do only the things that come first, and find his satisfaction in having done them well.

A still further form of concentration is demanded of the parish minister who would use his time wisely. He must discriminate between the major and the minor duties in each day's work. Right here lies a certain differentiation between the work of the minister and of other professional and business men. These go at once each morning to their major tasks. The lawyer has his work all laid out for him when he reaches his office. The doctor goes straight to the hospital, the teacher to the school, the business man to his affairs. But since the minister is not summoned immediately and perforce to his main duty, the danger lies that he will concern himself with other necessary but minor matters instead of coming to grips at once with his hardest work. There are domestic duties to be attended to because he remains in the home instead of walking right out of it. There are letters to be written, parish lists to be corrected, telephone calls to make, or an errand or two. Thus the precious hours which should be devoted to hard intellectual work are invaded and occupied by these lesser matters. He keeps busy all the time, and what he is busy about has its certain importance, but it is not of chief importance. Hence he must have the courage to sweep all these aside and avoid a certain dissipation of energy, a frittering of strength, a loss of discipline in the use of his mental powers.[1] Lesser matters must not be allowed to occupy the highest stations. They must not be elevated to a position that does not belong to them. There must be this deliberate assignment of what is to be done each day in the order of its importance.

Most men find that they can do their best intensive and constructive work in the morning when the mind is fresh and keen. This is so true that there are many who cannot think deeply, construct sermons and addresses, write or study with application and industry except during the morning hours. Hence the time between breakfast and luncheon they keep sacred to this kind of work. They avoid all morning appointments, decline invitations to go here or there, to do this or that. Indeed, they are seldom seen on the streets during the morning. They apply themselves for these four hours to severe mental work. For without it they cannot maintain a high level of intellectual and spiritual performance.

[1] Many years ago Sir William Robertson Nicoll wrote an article for ministers in *The British Weekly*. Its title was: "Mr. Fritterday."

At this point a problem arises. Shall a minister insist that he be not interrupted during these hours? Shall he see people who come to him for one cause or another? Some ministers decline to receive morning callers. Others are not to be found during the morning either at their homes or parish houses. They rent a room the location of which is unknown to all but members of the family and they are never disturbed except on emergency. It is a question, however, whether a parish minister has a right to such seclusion. After all that has been said, still it remains true that intellectual interests are not his highest interests. The making of a sermon is not his most imperative task. His supreme concern always is to help a human soul at the hour of its need. And that hour may fall in the morning. From this point of view a parish minister should always be accessible. No barriers should exist at any time between him and human beings. If they need him, he should be available at the time of their need. It can be said in sheer literalness of the true parish minister that he cannot be bothered for the simple reason that it is his blessed business to be bothered. He stands ready to sacrifice anything: time, strength, convenience, comfort, to help at any time a human soul. The minister who feels that anything is more important than this is disqualified to be a minister.

Thus what is called an interruption may not really be an interruption to him at all. An interruption is an intrusion upon one's proper task by something that is not relevant to it. But the proper task for the minister may not be what seems to be his work at the moment, but may lie in what appears to be the intrusion. When Peter was thinking about his vision, we read, three men called. But the call of those three men was not an interruption, rather it was his supreme opportunity. And a higher duty may present itself to the minister at any hour in the morning than the best work which he may then be doing.

Many people will make appointments in advance, but some will act on impulse, others in emergencies. And one can never know when these will arrive. Some, who have no legitimate claim on the minister's time, may be courteously deflected at the door. Still, he will see anyone who asks to see him at any time. If it turn out to be an honest book-agent, a vendor of laces or oil-burners, he will know how to terminate the interview gently and briefly. But he will not miss the chance of seeing those who really need him. Neither will he be guilty of the gross impropriety of having them asked to give their name or state their errand. That may do for a business executive, but not for a priest. Happy the minister who has learned that interruptions are his job. Unhappy the one to whom they remain interruptions. A. C. Benson was once informed by a colleague of his at Cambridge that an undergraduate wanted to consult him. "Why does he not come to see me?" "He would like to, but he is afraid that he might intrude." To which Benson replied: "I do not relish a compliment to my industry at the expense of my humanity."

Of course interruptions cost something. The point is that we usually assume that the so-called interruptions are inferior to the thing interrupted. Yet often the opposite is true. And the inevitable cost of lost momentum, the necessity of discovering and picking up again the thread of one's ideas, the effort to get the mental machinery at work once more, can be greatly reduced by one who avoids irritability and learns quickly to readjust himself to his task. Only those who are keen, capable, methodical and thorough know the dangers to the mental processes involved in these "interruptions." Thus to accept them cheerfully, meet the emergency competently, and quickly to readjust oneself to the task one had laid aside — this is a fine test of a high-grade soul.

Evidently the minister must use much wisdom, control, and courage in the use he makes of his time. In a word, in this, as in all else, he must be the artist. He makes due time allowances: he will not start for an appointment just in time to meet it only to be detained at the last moment; he will not plan a piece of work so that it shall be ready precisely when it is due only to be deprived of time that he had counted upon and thus fail to have it ready. Rather he will allow for these delays and possible accidents to his time-table and by this act of courage and wisdom avoid rush, irritability and tardiness. "There are some (people), and they are nearly always those who have achieved success, who seem to have time for practically everything. Nothing disturbs them. They are always cheerful and courteous. Their capacious lives, already containing many interests, seem always to have space for more. They have the capacity for standing a series of interruptions which would drive most people distracted. And each day of their lives ends with far more business done and pleasure experienced than others achieve in a week." Get at the heart of this, and one discovers the lofty courage with which without any loss of time they attack their work, utilize each moment at their disposal, and know how to conserve their nervous energy by the avoidance of strain and tension.

The utilization of his spare moments is often all that the busiest minister needs in order to remedy the worst defects in his character and performance. To gather up carefully the broken bits of one's time is the simple but efficient cure for the chronic lack of time which in strenuous days is the complaint of all. If we watch the most efficient people we know, we will find that they never waste time, the most precious commodity which we possess. They literally "give every flying minute something to [think or do]." Thus they learn how to master time rather than be mastered by it. The biographer of Dr. William Osler has written of him: "He utilized every minute of his time. On railway, in tramway, book and pencil were ever in his hand and wherever he was the happy thought was noted down. His power to hold the mastery of his time was remarkable. He escaped [from people] as by magic, but so graciously, so engagingly that despair though one might, one could hardly be irritated. No one could speak consecutively to Osler against his will. In his course of life he was more regular and systematic than words can tell. His cheerfulness and equanimity were surprising. Nothing ruffled his wonderful temper." [2] Here is high romance in the sphere of daily living.

[2] Harvey Cushing, *Life of Sir William Osler*, Vol. I, pp. 431, 432, 157, 158. Oxford University Press, publishers.

Are There Not Twelve Hours in the Day?

The rigid economy of time, it will be noticed, is here combined with a certain resiliency, ease, good humor. There is no hint of strain or irritability. "One of the surest marks of greatness," Robert Louis Stevenson has written, "is accessibility and the appearance of having an unstinted allowance of time. Extreme busyness, whether at school or college, kirk or market, is a symptom of deficient vitality; and a faculty for idleness implies a catholic appetite and a strong sense of personal identity." [3] This "faculty for idleness" is not a contradiction of the faculty of concentration. Rather it is the complement of it. The capacity to relax, to relieve muscular and nervous tension, to unburden oneself, is as important as the ability to work with promptness and energy. Only by acquiring both does one learn to use his time aright.

Dr. Richard C. Cabot understood the value of spare moments and never wasted them. Coming out of the hospital one day he met a friend. "Coming along?" he inquired. "Yes," answered the other, "in five minutes." "Oh, that is too bad," replied the doctor, "I must go now." Yet on the other hand he understood the importance of relaxation. In an article entitled "How to Avoid the Breathless Habit," he wrote: "The best oarsman rests between each stroke. The most efficient social worker will have a vacation every day." [4] Work unrelieved by relaxation, activity without repose is the only kind of work that kills. What is imperatively demanded is pause, retirement, the happy

[3] *Virginibus Puerisque,* "An Apology for Idlers," p. 90. Charles Scribners' Sons, publishers.
[4] *Charities and the Commons, Vol. 20, pp. 320–322.*

faculty of tossing off one's cares and letting the inward life renew itself.

If one opens the Gospels and studies the daily life of Jesus, one will be impressed with the way in which he mastered and controlled the time-element in his life. Never was a human life more beset with clamorous duty. Never was pressure greater, and "interruptions" were almost an hourly occurrence. Yet there is no indication to be found on the Gospel pages of haste, distraction, or impatience. Rather there is a certain atmosphere of serenity and of leisureliness. His life was not one of diminishing but of increasing activity. Yet his strength was always equal to his task. What was the secret of such a life that was filled with activity yet was always composed?

We discover for one thing that he never lived beyond his strength. He lived well within himself. He recognized the limitations of his human powers. He set definite limits to his work and he rigidly kept within them. He was not in haste, for he sought to do only what within the compass of each day of his life he was able to do. "Are there not twelve hours in the day?" He would use those hours and thus finish the work that was given him that day to do. "Interruptions" were not impertinent invasions alien to his task; rather they were his task. They did not deflect him from his main purpose. For he came for the precise purpose of saving those who called to him for help. And in the crowded life of Jesus we observe obedience to the law of rhythm and of change. Activity was followed by rest. After a day of strenuous labor, he went apart by himself. He imposed on himself hours when he retired within himself and allowed the tides of the spirit to flow in again and fill his soul with renewed energy and strength.

It is as the disciple of Jesus who has been summoned by his master to preach the gospel, heal the sick, and minister in his name learns the high strategy of Jesus in the employment of his time that he labors with efficiency and serenity, and, the day's work over, goes to his rest in peace.

CHAPTER 6

A Workman that Needeth Not to Be Ashamed

THE minister will face his total task with the romantic resolve that he will do everything he has to do, if not as well as it can be done, at least as well as he can do it. *Tout bien ou rien* will be his motto. He may be hurried, even harried, but careless or slovenly never. He puts character into every detail of his work, which is thus the expression of himself. Distasteful tasks he performs promptly and with thoroughness. It has been said that an educated man is one who, if he has two things to do, one of which he loathes and the other of which he loves, always does the one he loathes first. Little duties are performed with the same exactness as important ones. He learns, as Emerson put it, that "the unremitting retention of simple and high sentiments in obscure duties is hardening the character to that temper which will work with honor, if need be, in the tumult or on the scaffold." In all things he is the good workman "that needeth not to be ashamed."

By thus doing well whatever he has to do, he transmutes routine duties into things of real beauty and meaning. Work that is done half-heartedly never yields one any satisfaction. That arrives only as one has taken the meanest task and made it shine like light. Since the half-doing of that which one dislikes never yields anything but disgust, the way to redeem it is to do it thoroughly and thus have the joy of producing something perfect in its kind. Charles Dickens once said: "Whatever I have tried to do in life, I have tried with all my heart to do well: Whatever I have devoted myself to, I have devoted myself to completely; in

great aims and in small I have been thoroughly in earnest."
And the old Wisdom writer put it more tersely: "Whatso-
ever thy hand findeth to do, do it with thy might."

These maxims find their illustration in every sphere
of human application, but they have particular pertinency
to the life of the parish minister. He is likely to find himself at the beginning of his ministry in a small and inconspicuous parish, which may seem to present scant opportunity for the exercise of his powers. In this he is
mistaken, for the smallest parish presents opportunities
beyond the powers of those most richly endowed. He could
labor there all his life and perform a work of vast significance. Some years ago visitors to Cadouin, a little
French village not far from Brantôme — they had come to
see some rich decorations in the cloister of the parish
church — found there an aged curé who had spent his life
in the place. They had to wait until he had finished in-
structing a class of catechumens. Then with pride the old
man pointed out and explained to them the rich carvings
and sculptures in the cloister. He had lived there for forty-
four years, declining offers of advancement to larger
parishes because he was so in love with the place. His am-
bitions were fully satisfied with what he found there. A
similar romantic estimate of the country parish in which
many a young man finds himself will cure him of any itch
for a "larger field" and fill him with deepest satisfaction
and gratitude for the work which there he finds given
him to do.

To it he will apply himself with all of his God-given
powers and exercise all the talents he possesses. His con-

gregation may be small and unlearned, but he will prepare his sermons with the utmost care and fashion them according to the needs of his people. The funds may be limited; all the more he will seek to have them used to the best advantage. The equipment may be poor; he will study how it may be improved. The parish may be composed of only a few hundred souls; he will remember that each one of these has its need of sacramental grace. The children may be few, yet not one of them but may grow beyond all human reckoning in character and influence. In a word, he idealizes the whole situation, sees in it the possibilities of spiritual romance, and devotes to it every capacity of mind and soul.

Thus he learns the essential technique of a spiritual ministry. Indeed there is a sense in which "pastoral care" can be learned not in a school of theology but only in the care of a parish. He acquires skill in the use of his tools; in methods of administration; in ways of the religious training of the young; in parish visitation. The smallest parish offers a minister an invaluable opportunity of learning his trade. And to the degree to which he devotes himself whole-heartedly and with interest and imagination to his work, does he acquire competency and efficiency. He becomes disciplined in every aspect of his task.

So also does he unconsciously prepare himself for the summons that may come to him for a position which cannot be more useful, but may be more prominent and lucrative. For while income is never an object to the true minister, inevitably it has its economic importance. The real way to step into a "larger field" is thoroughly to cultivate the smaller one. The minister who is wanted is the one who has proved that he can do good work. The one who feels that his parish is so small that it does not deserve his best efforts, who regards it only as a stepping-stone, and almost at once looks for what he calls a better chance, never gets very far. But the man who devotes himself with energy, imagination, and interest to the parish that is his prepares for future opportunities which often disclose themselves only by force of zeal and thoroughness. The small task often can be marvelously transformed into an open way if a man performs it with competency. By putting character into work, a man builds up force in himself and sets influences into motion which carry him far on the road he wishes to travel. The good workman inevitably becomes known and is always in demand. It is true that competent men have served small parishes for many years. A Harvard University professor who had lectured at a State Conference composed almost exclusively of ministers of rural parishes, said that his experience had given him new respect for the ministry. These men, he declared, were intellectually the equal of any body of men he had ever addressed. It does not always happen that competency has its visible rewards. Yet nothing short of it ever qualifies for advancement in the ministry.

Paul advised Timothy to "train himself for the religious life." [1] The phrase is inclusive. It involves the essential asceticism necessary to keep the moral fiber firm. It demands an unremitting mental discipline. One's mind must not be allowed to become sluggish, flabby, or indolent. Hard

[1] *I Timothy 4:8* (Goodspeed's translation).

food, we are told, is good for the teeth. But some ministers lose their mental teeth before they are thirty. They will neither bite on a new idea nor chew an uncomfortable fact. It is so much easier to read books that reflect their own opinions than to wrestle with ideas foreign to their pre-dispositions or struggle to do justice to notions that offend their prejudices. They do not know how to think, for real thinking is to bring the mind resolutely to bear upon something which can be understood and mastered only by mental effort and application.

Hence the minister will do well to read modern heretical literature and confront ideas which contradict his own innate convictions. Always, too, he will have before him some study which has nothing whatever to do with the preparation of sermons or addresses. These call for the application of religious truth to human need. But there is a different use of the mind: the discovery of truth itself; the pitting of one's wits against difficult mental problems; in a word, intellectual discipline. And this the wise minister will not neglect. He will map out for himself a thorough course of reading, whether in philosophy, the social sciences, or Biblical history and criticism. A few books will always be in front of him to guide him. And to these extra-ecclesiastical studies he will give many hours. The minister whose mental processes are devoted exclusively to the preparation of sermons is not training himself, as he should, for the religious life.

The minister, then, who is resolved to be a good work-man will see that nothing escapes his eye or the impress of his spirit. The whole of his parish work will reflect his ideals, his culture, his character. This involves careful study of method, firm knowledge of principles, and rigorous holding to the highest ideals. He will begin with the church property. The buildings may not be modern or elaborate, but he will insist that they be kept neat, clean, and orderly. One can get a clue to the workmanship of a minister the moment one enters his church or parish house. If one sees frayed carpets, shabby hymnbooks, a choir loft in disorder, chairs in disrepair, an untidy office or study, all of this reveals lack of care and absence of ideals. The true minister is scrupulous in these matters. He makes a comrade of his sexton and imbues him with his own ideals. He has a committee of women whose duty it is to care for the house of God as they do for their own homes. He enlists the service of children, who are taught to pick up hymnbooks from the floor, remove paper from the lawns or grounds, and to take a pride in the appearance of their church. He will tolerate no carelessness in the use of bulletin boards or the posting of any announcements without approval. He may well make a tour of the entire property once a week to see that wash rooms are kept clean and any broken furniture is removed. When once this passion for order is created, it spreads. Thus the minister proves himself to be a good workman.

Parish organization will demand a minister's constant attention. Here he proves himself to be a good business executive. There may be too many organizations; he will see that they are consolidated. Some of them may have served their purpose, but are no longer needed; they will be discontinued. New methods of parish administration are constantly being put forward. He will keep abreast of these and see that they are incorporated in the church organization which will present an aspect as modern and well-knit as any business concern in the community. In all of this he will take pride. He will be a constant parish builder, never satisfied with antiquated methods, always alert to new ideas.

In the ordering of the parish life, he will see that the fundamentally religious function of the church is never lost sight of. What goes on in the way of social activities in the parish house is never given such importance and prominence that it over-tops what goes on in the sanctuary. People must be drawn to the church primarily because of the spiritual gifts it offers them. The church is degraded if people are attracted to it primarily by its program of social events or activities. These have their place, but that place is secondary and must be so kept. The function of the parish house is to provide a center for human fellowship, social acquaintance, and common activities for people who have become members of a spiritual household for spiritual ends. And everything that goes on in the parish house will be permeated with spiritual purpose. The purely secular demand for entertainment and amusement is met elsewhere. Within the life of the church one is made aware of the operation of spiritual ideas in comradeship and of a certain type of idealism in all forms of entertainment. There must be a difference felt, even if it cannot be wholly defined. Here is a sphere of influence in which the minister can bring to bear the truest and highest ideals. It is an important element in the church's education of its youth.

In few departments of church work has greater progress been made in recent years than in that of church music. A steady and persistent educational program has been going forward for some time, fostered by church leaders and the musical profession. A considerable and helpful literature on the subject has been published.[2] As a result the type of music sung both by congregations and church choirs has been immeasurably improved. It is not at all the exception today in even the smaller and rural churches to hear music of a high order sung by well-trained choirs. The substitution of a voluntary chorus for the professional quartette has in itself been a vast gain. And the training of the youth and children of the Church in choral singing has been an invaluable element in their religious training.

In all of this the parish minister will have a personal and lively interest. It used to be said that the authority and influence of the minister stopped at the choir loft. If that is true today it is the minister's fault alone. The choir master or organist is by no means as temperamental and jealous of his own rights and prerogatives as he is often represented to be. On the contrary, he is usually eager to cooperate with the minister and is ready to adapt his work to the ideals of worship which the minister cherishes. The two men should work together to achieve the

[2] The reader is referred to *Music in Worship* by Joseph N. Ashton. Pilgrim Press, 1942.

spiritual ends which each, in his own way, is seeking to attain.

For this it is not necessary that the minister should be a trained musician or be what is called "musical." But he should have and can readily acquire a knowledge of the place and function of music in the worship of the Church. He will know that the opening anthem will be one of praise; that the choir number in the middle of the service will be devotional in character and that the music should be adapted not to the sermon but to the rotation of the church year and of the natural seasons. He will see that the service is not overburdened or lengthened unduly by choir singing; that responses to prayers are carefully selected and sung. He will visit his choirs at their rehearsals and have quiet talks with the singers, reminding them of the importance of their work, telling them how much he depends upon them. He will speak of church decorum and remind them that they are in full view of the congregation. He will ask that they lead the congregation strongly in the singing of the hymns. He may even draw up a printed list of suggestions to put into their hands and make this the basis of his choir talks. Choirs respond gladly to this creation of a spiritual bond between the singers and the minister.

The congregation will be encouraged by every means in the minister's power to join heartily in the hymn-singing. Perhaps no witness of the worshiping church is more effective than this. Right here, however, a problem projects itself. The repertory of familiar hymns which the whole congregation can easily sing is very brief. In order that the congregation shall sing heartily, shall the minister limit his selection to the hymns "which everybody knows"? Many ministers do this and thus neglect a whole body of noble hymns which are to be found in every hymnbook. Some ministers rarely use more than half a hundred hymns in a collection of four or five hundred at their disposal. Thus the congregation is deprived of much fine hymnody, the use of which would enrich their religious culture. A way out of this difficulty is to choose four or five hymns each parish year which are not familiar, but have enduring worth; to inform the congregation that they will be sung repeatedly during the year and invite their cooperation. The people will respond eagerly, and gradually the number of hymns in which the congregation can joyfully unite in singing will be increased.

In such ways as these the minister can use his influence in the musical department of his church. And his rewards will be rich.

It is regrettable that the minister should have much responsibility for church finances. Surely here is a task which should rest squarely upon the shoulders of laymen. The minister has enough else to do, without being worried about the raising of funds. In the old days when most church organizations were composed of two bodies, the spiritual and the secular, and all monies necessary for church expenses were raised by the method of pew rentals, the minister was relieved of much responsibility for financing the church. Indeed, he was not supposed to know much about it. Today, however, when churches are incorporated and when pew-rentals have been largely abandoned, the whole matter of finances is put into the hands of a governing board, by whatever name it may be called, of which the minister is a member and usually the chairman. Hence it is inevitable that he should have intimate knowledge of and a certain measure of responsibility for the budgets for both benevolent objects and parish expenses, and for the methods for raising the desired sums. A woman once said: "I should think that the time for drawing up budgets and arranging for the 'every-member canvass' would be an annual nightmare for the minister." To a certain extent it often is.

Laymen, if they are wise, will seek to lessen the minister's burden at this point in every possible way. They will assure the minister that this is their job. They will not expect him to concern himself about its details. And ministers, if they are wise, will limit their contribution to this cause to its spiritual aspects. Nothing is more deadening to the spiritual life of a church than reiterated exhortations by the minister for a "large offering" or the frequent projection of finances to the attention of the congregation. If financial statements must be made, it is far better that this be done by a layman. The minister's duty is to seek, not only once a year when the annual canvass is made, but on different occasions, to emphasize the idea of stewardship as the Christian's responsibility and privilege; to instruct his people in the spiritual meanings that underlie one's use of his money; to point out the necessity for regular and proportionate giving as part of one's religious life and experience; in a word, to present the Bible doctrine of the offering as worship. Thus the ground will be prepared and cultivated, made rich and responsive. There lies his peculiar and solitary task. Above all, he will be concerned for the missionary interest and enthusiasm of his congregation, that the amounts spent on parish expenses shall not be wholly out of proportion to those used for the propagation of the gospel to the ends of the earth. Here he will speak with conviction and passion. The missionary interest of any church is in direct proportion to the missionary zeal of the parish minister.

These, then, are spheres of activity in which the parish minister can prove himself to be a good workman. Instead of being dull and prosaic tasks, they present themselves to his mind as opportunities for the exercise of a high degree of spiritual imagination. They have their own romantic interest and are permeated with an idealism which transforms them into things of brightness and beauty. Hence he finds a certain inward joy in the doing of them and because he does them well, he has the secret satisfaction of the "workman that needeth not to be ashamed."

CHAPTER 7

A Sower Went Forth to Sow

✠ ✠ ✠ ✠ ✠ ✠ ✠

THE varied tasks of the parish minister often seem to be different and unrelated forms of activity. They are, so it appears, separate departments from one to another of which he must pass. It is as if he were doing four or five distinct kinds of work at the same time. He must prepare his sermons; he must make his pastoral visits; he must care for his church school and other organizations; he must manage his parish affairs. There is no apparent unity in these divergent and often competing interests. Hence he finds himself going from one to the other, seeking to adjust himself to the special demands of each and to find time for them all.

As a matter of fact, all these forms of activity are but different aspects of a single task. The same principle runs through them all. The same motive lies beneath them. They are all directed to the same end. Let a minister once grasp what his sole purpose and mission is, and his work will present itself to him as a unity. He is not doing different things in different ways; he is doing the same thing in the same way. The scene may alter, but his purpose and his method do not change.

In the familiar parable of the sower we find expressed this identity of the minister's task in its varied aspects. It is one of the simplest of the parables. The scholars, for once, all agree on its interpretation. The seed is the word, the grace, the life of God; the soil is the heart of man; the sower is the Son of God and those whom God's Son has called to be the sons of God. The teaching of the parable is twofold. It tells us that our mission in life is to be good sowers of the seed. It reminds us that not all the seed we sow will fall into good ground and bring forth much fruit. Some of it will not bring forth any fruit at all. Yet some of it will fall in rich soil, unknown perhaps to ourselves, and bring forth an abundant harvest.

Now the sowing of seed is the most romantic process of which we have any knowledge. It is at once the simplest and yet the most mysterious. The seed is a miracle, containing within itself invisible energies capable of producing the bewildering beauty of the flowers, rich and luscious fruits, the wheat and corn by which we live. The process by which this is done is a mystery. By what alchemy of nature the powers in the seed cooperate with those in the soil to produce these results we do not know. All that man can do is to put the seed in the soil, prepared to receive it, and wait for the harvest. And that is all that the Son of God and the sons of God can do. Whether the seed will spring up, where it will spring up and when — all that lies beyond one's knowledge. His task is to sow the seed and to sow it as freely, as broadly as he can. To God belongs the harvest. The one question which ministers of Jesus Christ have to ask themselves is whether the picture of that Galilean peasant striding across his field sowing the seed as carefully and plentifully as he can, is true of them. Are they doing just that, only that, day by day and every day? When they get up and go about their day's work, whatever its particular tasks may be, can it be said of them: "Behold, a sower goes forth to sow"?

It is true, of course, that we are sowing whether we realize it or not. Unconsciously we are leaving impressions on the minds of others simply by what we are or are not; by what we say or leave unsaid; by what we do or leave undone; by our reserves and reticences as well as by our deliberate acts. The deductions people are drawing daily from our casual words, appearance, deportment that we know nothing about — this is our unconscious sowing. One of the most haunting questions in life, if we stop to reflect on it, concerns the effect upon others of this unconscious sowing of ourselves. Real influence cannot be tabulated. It is the steady persistent power of what we are. George Adam Smith said that his task of writing the life of Henry Drummond was like trying to write the history of a fragrance. What is more elusive yet more pervasive than a fragrance? Drummond did more good by what he was than by anything he did. He was once asked by a woman to visit her husband who was dying. She wanted him to "have a breath of Drummond about him" before he died.

Or consider Thomas Chalmers, a man venerated by high and low. He was a powerful preacher, one of the most eminent that even Scotland has produced. He exercised a great influence by his sermons, his preaching, his efforts at social betterment. Yet after one has rendered account of all this, one has not begun to touch the secret of his real influence. It has been said of him that "for a decade before he died, he had passed beyond the sphere of criticism into that of universal homage. He seemed unconscious of it and went on his way with what Carlyle called his heavenly industries, never giving a thought to the chorus of praises sounding round him every day. He was recognized as a universal benediction by the simple but mighty fact of his human excellence." What seed did these men sow just by what they were! The same seed may any minister sow who has within him the indubitable, authentic, eloquent spirit of Jesus. A parish minister should walk close to God before he walks out into the life of his parish. For what he is, to paraphrase Emerson, will speak louder than anything which he says or does.

When the minister goes out about his task, whatever his special duties may be, always he remembers that his identical mission is to sow the seeds of God's grace in the human heart. Within them are compacted all kinds of revolutionary and romantic possibilities. If he can plant them in the soil of one human soul, he has done a work beyond all computation. How it would transform what seem to be the routine tasks of each day if he went about it with that one idea in mind; if taking account of his activity in whatever sphere it were exercised, others would say of him: "Just look at that man going forth to sow."

George Matheson in his too little-known book *Spiritual Development of St. Paul* [1] has suggested an interpretation which gives fresh and helpful meaning to the familiar words in the great resurrection chapter in First Corinthians: "It is sown in corruption; it is raised in incorruption: it is sown in dishonour; it is raised in glory: it is sown in weakness; it is raised in power." To what, he has asked, does the word "it" refer? Not, as commonly

[1] E. R. Herrick and Company, N. Y., pp. 156–159.

83

supposed, to the human body. Grammatically the antecedent of "it" is not the body but the resurrection principle itself. The Apostle "is not speaking of the gradations through which the body passes, but of the gradations through which resurrection passes." The thing that is sown is not the body and the place in which the sowing is done is not the ground. The thing that is sown is the seed of the resurrection. And the place where that divine seed is planted is the human heart just as it is — corruptible, dishonorable, weak.

"The life of Christ in the soul has its beginnings in great humiliation. . . . Instead of waiting for the purification of the natural man, [it] descends into the natural man in his present unpurified condition. It does not tarry till the house is . . . swept and garnished; it comes down into the house while it is yet full of corruption, uncleansed, unbeautified. . . . The seed which is sown in it is a principle of vitality which has emptied itself into humiliation, which has condescended to dwell amid conditions which are foreign to its own nature. . . . It has done in the soul what the Son of Man did in the world, poured out its native glory, and assumed a servant's form." But if that was the beginning, it was not the conclusion. The divine seed is sown in corruption, but it is raised in incorruption; it is sown in dishonor, but it is raised in glory; it is sown in weakness, but it is raised in power. And Christian history is filled with illustrations of the romantic process by which frail and dishonorable human lives have, by the operation within them of the revolutionary powers of the seed of the divine life, known their resurrection into lives of beauty and glory and power.

It is the ambition of the parish minister to see that this revolutionary process finds its illustration in the lives of those who are committed to his charge. Hence his most sacred task is to cause this divine seed to be planted in human hearts by all the care, diligence, and skill that he can exercise. In all that he does, this is the one dominating motive. It runs through every phase of his activity. It binds all of his separate duties together into a living and spiritual whole.

When he preaches, he scatters the living seed over his congregation with the hope, prayer, and expectation that some of it will fall into responsive soil and take root. True preaching has for its ultimate purpose the planting of the grace of God in human hearts. The one idea which the preacher holds before him is not to impart information, to seek to interest or entertain, or even to exhort. Rather he seeks to take a handful of seed and to sow it as carefully as he can. It must be good seed, rich in the fructifying powers of the divine life, without too much admixture either of intellectualism or secularism. It must be sown with every regard for the capacities, the needs, the employments of his hearers. It must have behind and within it the love of the preacher. It must be bathed in prayer. If preaching could always be conceived as the opportunity for sowing the seed, it would often be more fruitful than it is.

When the minister goes about the task of pastoral visitation, he carries the same idea with him. It is now the individual or the family group with which he has to deal.

But his one idea when he enters a home is to see if, before he leaves it, he can put some of this divine seed into the hearts of those who live there: of courage, faith, charity, of penitence, it may be, and hope. It is a beautiful and romantic business. In matters of parish organization and detail, the same idea dominates and controls. Here one seeks to sow the seeds of tolerance, cooperation, and good will. Every church should be a training school in these virtues for the lack of which so much goes awry in the outer world. And in his most casual meetings with individuals, always the instinct of this seed-sowing operates. It may be just a word of friendliness, a little act of courtesy or helpfulness. Yet these are seeds sown in passing and often they find lodgment in someone's heart and do good beyond all knowing. They help to freshen and brighten life; they leave behind them a sense of happiness. How numberless are the opportunities thus granted the parish minister for sowing God's seed in human lives! Think of one day of such sowing. Then multiply these days over the years and try to compass the extent and depth of influence which may belong to any minister of Jesus Christ. Its outgoings may be literally to the ends of the world.

When he has sown his seed as best he can, his work is done. His duty is over. True, he will watch over it, tend it, cultivate it as best he may, but the harvest belongs to God. The sower knows that some, perhaps much, of the seed that he has sown will not spring up at all. Just as a thousand influences can prevent the seeds which are put into the ground from taking root, just so invisible forces over which he has no control can prevent the seed which the most loving care has sown in human hearts from bearing visible fruit. Our parable makes that plain also. Some of the seed will fall on hard ground, on hearts which because of exclusive devotion to material interests are rendered impervious to any form of spiritual impression. Some of this seed will fall on thin soil, on hearts which are impulsively receptive, but soft and without tenacity of purpose. This is one of the most common kinds of soil. Church membership books are filled with the names of those who received the seed with joy, but which, because there was no root to it, soon withered away. Again there is the soil that is neither too hard nor too thin, but too crowded. The place where the seed fell was preoccupied. And into such crowded lives much good spiritual seed will fall helpless, destined in advance to early death. Such is the teaching of Jesus himself.

Thus for all of this the minister is not responsible. He knows that these kinds of soil exist all around his field. Much of the seed he sows may not come up at all. Much of it may spring up a little, but not to fruition. That he understands. It was so in Jesus' day and it is so in our day. But that is not the affair of the sower. His task is to sow as well as he can. He proceeds in no niggardly fashion. He strides across his field scattering the seed broadcast. The results belong to God.

If workers for God would only remember where lie the limits of their responsibility, they would be saved from much discouragement. Discouragement comes from looking for results, immediate results, results from all the seed which one has sown. Yet this one has no right to expect. Experts in agriculture remind discouraged farmers that they must look for a good crop from only one cut of three sowings. The faithful sower of spiritual seed will make the same discovery. No man has been long in the ministry without noting how illogical is the relation between effort and result. Sometimes when he has tried his hardest and seems to himself to have done his best work, the results are disappointingly meager. At other times when he is not aware that he has been doing good work at all, he is bewildered by the rich rewards of his labor. "The seed springeth up, he knoweth not how. For the earth bringeth forth fruit of herself." [2] The harvest is unpredictable.

Thus, the minister will always fix his eyes on the fact and duty of his sowing. He will not reckon the value of his work by its visible results. Here is where many go wrong. They are keen on results. Hence if the spiritual seed which they have tried to sow does not produce these results, they must try other means. The pews must be filled up. If spiritual preaching will not fill them up, then they must try other forms of preaching that will. New members of the church must be added to its rolls. They must make a good showing in the denominational yearbook. Hence, all must be accepted who are willing to be enrolled on any terms or no terms at all. One must not look too closely for signs that the divine seed has entered their hearts. Numbers are the thing.

[2] *Mark 4:27, 28.*

Here is a temptation which every true minister will resist with all his soul. Numbers are not the thing. They did not bulk largely in the mind of Jesus. He was not eager for what we call "results." He allowed the rich young man to go away, and Jesus was more sorrowful than he. But only one who had made the full surrender of his life to God could enroll himself among his disciples. What we call "results" often have no significance whatever. Because a church is crowded it does not follow that any lasting good is being done there. The minister may point to a long list of new members, yet have failed to sow seed that shall spring up thirty or sixty or a hundredfold. Let him fix his eyes on his sowing. In season and out of season, let him be a faithful sower of the seed. That and that alone is his responsibility. The results he must leave to God.

For, and here lies the romance of his work, some of this seed, and often where he least looks for it, will fall into good and honest hearts and bring forth wonderful fruits of the spirit. And he can never know when or where this miracle will happen. Years ago there was an old minister in Manchester, England, who thought that he ought to resign because only one boy as the result of a year of faithful sowing of the seed presented himself for church membership. When the minister was asked by the church officers if he knew anything about the boy, he admitted that he did not. But that boy's name was Robert Moffat, pioneer missionary to Africa, whose daughter married David Livingstone. All of the great pioneer missionaries here in America came out of small country churches: [3] Adoniram Judson, Samuel Nott, Samuel New-ell, Luther Rice. Three families whose names have become household words in missionary history — the Humes, the Fairbanks's, the Howlands — all came from small communities. What results were these to the faithful sowing of the seed! Some of the outstanding men and women in American life have come out of small country churches. The State of Maine is a rural state of small towns and villages. Yet it has furnished more mental timber to the nation in proportion to the population than any other state in the Union: men and women who have been bred and reborn in country churches, whose ministers have gone right on sowing the seed in the face of every discouragement. Every minister who does the same thing has the glad surprise of beholding someone whose life presented the appearance of being unlikely soil bringing forth fruit in abundance. Sowing the seed is indeed the most romantic task in the world.

Sometimes one sees a flower growing in a bit of earth in rocky soil or in a cranny in a wall. A good seed has chanced to fall there; the soil has taken it into itself and there it grows into beauty. Thus we can sow in hope and faith. Much seed may fall on hard, on thin, on crowded soil and not bring forth fruit at all. But some of it will fall into good ground and we shall marvel at the harvest.

"I watched," a modern author has written, "an Italian peasant near Spello in the Umbian Valley sowing his seed in his tiny field broadcast with a primitive and splen-

[3]. See article "The World's Debt to Country Churches" by Cornelius H. Patton, *Missionary Herald*, February, 1921.

did gesture. And, having made an end of his work, in a corner of his field he knelt and prayed to God. . . . The corn which he sowed shall live again if God will, grow and be green, swept by the wind, dried with the sun and golden in the summer heat. In the cool night under the stars it is watched over, then reaped with labor and with joy. Happy in the fields, how shall I attain to his simplicity?"

Let one hang beside his bed a photograph or engraving of Millet's well-known painting, "The Sower" and take its lesson to his heart. Every morning let him look at it and say to himself: "I must sow some good seed today." When the day is over, let him look at it again. "Have I sown good seed this day?" And if he has, he, too, will kneel and pray to God to bless it. Then he may feel that his work has been done.

CHAPTER 8

The Pearl of Great Price

✛   ✛   ✛   ✛   ✛   ✛   ✛

THE little parable of the Pearl of Great Price has been uniformly interpreted by scholars, commentators, preachers, and the average Bible reader. The pearl is the gospel, finding which men are, or should be, ready to sell all that they have that they may purchase it for themselves. A closer examination of the parable, however, reveals a different interpretation which contains a profound truth essential to the redemptive work of the Christian ministry.

Reviewing the other parables contained in this thirteenth chapter of Matthew's Gospel, we discover that in each one Christ himself was the actor. It was he who went forth to sow, who planted the grain of mustard seed, who cast his net into the sea. Why, then, should not he be the merchant seeking goodly pearls? And if Christ be the merchant, then what is the pearl? The question answers itself. What was it that the Son of Man came to seek and to save? The sinner and the lost, the beggar and the outcast, the lowest and the most unfortunate of men. These were the reasons for his ministry on earth. These were his pearls, to purchase which he divested himself of all that he had.

Pearls then as now were rare and precious gems. Every one in that Galilean crowd to whom Jesus spoke knew what was meant by a pearl of great price. And here was Jesus telling them that these broken bits of humanity, these lepers and lunatics, these apparently worthless human objects, these vagrant children who got into every-

94

body's way, these nameless nobodies — these were his pearls of great price.

See, too, how beautifully the parable lends itself to this interpretation of it. The pearls, as we all know, lie in the depths. To get the best pearls, divers must go to the bottom. Even so, the Son of Man humbled himself and became obedient unto death, descended into the lowest parts of the earth, into the depths of our human humiliation that he might find his pearls of greatest price. Can we grasp the breath-taking meaning of this precious parable thus understood? It means nothing less than that the human spirits dwelling in the degraded body of one victim of drink and lust, a loathsome member of the gutter population of one of our great cities, is Jesus' pearl of great price.

Not long ago a young girl was committed to the reformatory. She was not more than a school girl, but she had not a shred of self-respect left. When she was brought into court, she was a pitiable spectacle. Dissipation and degradation had taken full toll of her. Her face was ashen pale from the habitual use of drugs. She stood absolutely indifferent to the proceedings and to her own fate. Mind had all but gone; will had all gone; self-respect had gone long ago. Stolid and impassive and without comprehension, she received her sentence. And after that? As a police reporter wrote on his pad, "just another bit of human flotsam, to be whirled around on the wheel of fate, until it disappears into nothingness." What was she worth? What was she good for? According to all human estimate, she was worth little or nothing. But according to this divine evaluation of our poor humanity, the girl just as she stood there was a pearl of great price, of such incalculable worth that it was just for her that the Lord of Glory sold all that he had that he might purchase her unto himself.

Here, then, is a romantic creed. One looks elsewhere in vain for such a divine estimate of the human soul at its worst. We do not find it in other ancient religions, nor do we find it in modern secular ethics. It certainly is not a human estimate, for it flies right in the face of the common-sense judgments of the world. Looked at through any other eyes than those of Jesus, these human derelicts are regarded as worthless and hopeless. But to the mind of Jesus every one of these bruised and broken fragments of humanity is of priceless worth. That is the gospel. If that is not true, Christianity is not true. Christianity lives and thrives by the majesty of its beliefs. And one of the most majestic of them all is this: that we see every human soul in the light that Jesus thought it so precious that he died for it.

Christianity's greatest triumphs have been won by the strength of this romantic dogma. It has given glory and potency and power to preaching. All through Christian history, preachers have confronted humanity at its worst and announced its possible redemption and salvation. Henry Drummond and Dwight L. Moody would talk to men whose lives resembled nothing so much as gutter sewage and point them to the snow-clad heights of holiness. It is one of the most glorious characteristics of the Salvation Army in its work for the outcasts, the destitute, the abandoned men and women of our day. Long after these victims of intemperance, disease, and vicious habits have ceased to believe in themselves, they begin again upon the unshakable foundation of another's faith in them as Jesus' pearls of great price. Faith in our fellow men has simply unpriced values. G. K. Chesterton once said of St. Francis that he treated the whole mob of men as if they were a lot of kings. Any preacher can face any man or any set of men in the light of this truth in the same way. No man can ever hold himself to be lost, if this parable be true.

When the Church has risen level to the implications of this romantic dogma, it has performed miracles that stand as shining landmarks in the moral history of the race. It has generated the passion which has lain behind the whole history of Christian missions and the glorious work of its missionaries who have gone to the ends of the earth to reclaim the lives of men and women and little children, sunk in misery, in squalor, in ignorance, and in sin. Because these are Jesus' pearls of great price, Carey went to India and Livingstone and Schweitzer to Africa, and Robert Morrison to China. This idea and none other is holding at their stations in the outposts of civilization today thousands of devoted Christian workers, and makes its irresistible appeal to others to enroll in the same sacrificial service of mankind. The truth within our little parable has been from the first and is today the "nerve of missions."

Again, all that is best in the Christian world today, all that we have most to be proud of — our humanitarian work for the outcasts, the incurables, the handicapped, the convict, the insane — is the product of the divine truth which lies at the heart of this parable. Or consider the relation of this dogma to the great ideals of social justice. Our little parable reminds us that the thing of supreme worth in the economy of God's universe is the life of his children. Above all material values there is the sanctity and preciousness of the soul of man. Well, that idea is simply packed with dynamite. It condemns any economic system, any organization of industry, which degrades the human soul and sets the acquisition of material wealth above the happiness and well-being of men and women and children, even as Jesus condemned those who harmed his pearls of great price.

Our parable is alive and at work in the world today and is seeking to mould it to its own image. Our parable may be called the charter and constitution of that new social order which is on its way. What form it will take, no man is prophet enough to say. But that the constitution of our human society will remain what it is, no thinking man believes. Behind the modern passion for social justice, social security, the abolition of poverty and unemployment, the well-being of the people as a whole lies this romantic creed of the infinite worth of every child of God. It has flashed its light across the dark pages of our social past and has won many victories. Many evils have been swept away. Many more remain. Yet these today are challenged by the social conscience generated by Jesus' divine valuation of the worth of man. This idea faces today the worst aspects of our social life, faces the vast iniquity and obscenity of the wholesale slaughter of human beings in war — a "lunatic anachronism" in our modern world. The ultimate salvation of God's children from the evils residing in the present organization of human society is to be found in the glorious dogma that every child of God is a pearl of great price for whom Jesus gave all that he had.

Thus it is of supreme importance that the minister of Jesus Christ get a firm grip on this fundamental truth. Upon his grasp of it will depend the redemptive power of his ministry. It will keep his missionary enthusiasm always at a white heat. He will never lose his missionary passion in all the discussion of missionary policies and methods that is going on in our day. The "re-thinking of missions" will never cause him to "err concerning the faith." Adjustments both on the field abroad and at the home base may be needed. Consolidation and unification of effort may be called for. Methods may change. But none of these, nor the pressure that may be brought upon him not to call too loudly for donations for missions because of the financial needs of his own parish, ever will cool his missionary ardor. He never forgets Jesus' pearls of great price.

Behold how many still are lying
   Bound in the dark-some prison-house of sin,
With none to tell them of the Saviour's dying,
   Or of the life he died for them to win.

'Tis thine to save from peril of perdition
   The souls for whom the Lord his life laid down:
Beware lest slothful to fulfill thy mission,
   Thou lose one jewel that should deck his crown.

Again, the parable will keep alive the social passion within the soul of the minister of Jesus Christ. Never will he acquiesce in the social evils that still defile the face of our civilization. His social conscience will always be keen and uncompromising. He will be a radical in the sense that he will carry to their roots the central religious ideas of Jesus of the sanctity of human life, of human brotherhood, of the unity of all mankind. He will insist that whatever defiles the souls and bodies of Jesus' pearls of great price is social sin. His preaching will be intensely spiritual, but its spirituality will possess, like that of his Master, a penetrating quality which will pierce through the shabbiness and hypocrisy of a religion which contents itself in outward form alone.

Once more, a firm hold on the truth embedded in this little parable will save the minister from what, as time goes on, will prove to be his most deadly temptation, the temptation to lose sight of the redemptive mission of the Church: its task and duty and mission to seek and to save the lost. One gets settled into his parish life, becomes immersed in his parish duties and accustomed to his parish routine. He has his flock to look after, his members to recruit, his children to instruct. Little by little, except he be on his guard, his evangelical passion will become cooled. He will forget the multitudes that are as sheep having no shepherd, the proletariat suffering from social injustice, in want, destitution and despair. There will be nothing within him to correspond to the passion of Jesus who left the ninety and nine and went in search of the one that was lost. Is not the besetting sin and temptation

17218

of the Church that it settle down into a narrow parochial-
ism, a self-satisfied ministry to those who naturally and of
their own accord associate themselves with it, and loses
sight of those ideals of devoted and sacrificial service which
alone give it the right to wear the name of its Lord? This
danger constantly threatens the life of the Church and the
moral life of its ministers. The realization of this drove
William Booth out of his Methodist ministry into the
slums; caused Silvester Horne to exchange his comfortable
suburban parish for one in the very heart of East London;
spurred Studdart Kennedy to throw open his parish rooms
to homeless vagrants that they might find warmth and
shelter; prompted William J. Dawson after an evening
service to lead his congregation out to the streets and
there preach the gospel to those who would never think
of entering within church walls. And the same passion
should possess the soul of every parish minister. The glory
of the ministry is a heart aflame, and that flame must never
die. Ministers today are being trained as hospital internes,
in psychiatry and personality problems. Why should they
not also be trained in "soul-saving" methods? Why should
they not spend some weeks before ordination in gospel missions? Why should they not interrupt for a time their
ministry to their comfortable and well-to-do congregations and work with those who, in the thick of our great
cities, are seeking to save the multitudes outside the reach
of organized ecclesiasticism? Would they not then return
to their parishes with the passion to save Jesus' pearls of
great price alive in their souls? For this must always be the
central passion of a true minister of Jesus Christ.

The Romance of the Ministry

Never then will he despair of any man. No one will ever assume to him the aspect of dull mediocrity or appear beyond redemption. Always he will see men even at their worst as one of Jesus' pearls of great price.

This is the deepest meaning of that clause in the Apostles' Creed which to many appears to be obscure and antiquated: "He descended into hell." Actually, it is one of the most eloquent words in it. It tells us that the Lord of Heaven went to the nethermost bottom of human need to find his pearls. The solemn words of the Creed sound like the tolling of a bell. It is Jesus going down: "Suffered under Pontius Pilate; crucified; dead; buried." Yet there are lower depths than death and burial. There is the hell of remorse, of unforgiven sin, of moral despair. Into that dark region of man's final hopelessness Jesus descended in search of his pearls. A young man once told his minister that he was in hell. "I know you are," replied the minister, "but you are not alone." "No," said the boy, "I guess that I have company all right." "You have," was the reply. "The company of the Lord Jesus Christ." "The Lord Jesus Christ! What does he know about where I am?" The minister slowly repeated the Creed: " 'He descended into hell.' Do you not see? He went down to where you are that you might find him there under you, to lift you out of the hell of your misery into life and manhood once more." The boy dropped on his knees and broke out sobbing. Jesus had found another of his pearls of great price. By the power of this majestic truth a minister of Jesus Christ can perform a romantic work for the lost souls of men.

CHAPTER 9

Fishers of Men

✠　　✠　　✠　　✠　　✠　　✠　　✠

I T is noteworthy, if we think of it at all, that Jesus chose fishermen to be his disciples. Peter and Andrew, James and John — the four leaders of the apostolic band — were men who plied their trade and sailed their boats on the blue waters of the Lake of Galilee; and it is probable that others of the Twelve followed the same calling. But why fishermen? This was not the ordinary vocation of the people of Palestine. Most of them were agriculturalists or shepherds or vineyardmen. Fishing was confined to a few. There was not much fishing to be done in that little land. There are no streams. No one can fish in the River Jordan, which is either a torrent in winter or a dry muddy stream in summer. The land is not dotted with lakes. There is only one: the stormy, squally Sea of Galilee under its overhanging hills. No one in Palestine would have dreamed of going deep-sea fishing in the Mediterranean, for they were not a sea-faring folk. Every voyage of which we have record in Scripture ended in shipwreck. For them, the sea was inhabited only by monsters and whales and leviathans. Perhaps the shepherd's calling was most deeply rooted in the people's past. The Bible is filled with references to the shepherd and the prophet is again and again pictured as an undershepherd of the Lord. But fishermen are seldom mentioned.

Why then did Jesus choose them? After his baptism, he found himself in Judea where were the shepherds and the vinedressers. A little further north were the fertile plains of Esdraelon, with the farmers at their tasks. Yet

104

Jesus passed them all by and went to the Lake of Galilee. He went to the one place in all the land where men could fish, and he chose them. It may have been, in part, because fishermen live an active life. The shepherd's life was essentially one of solitude. The farmer was alone on his acres. But the fisherman was in the midst of things. The modern traveler to the Lake of Tiberias finds him there just as Jesus did, in the center of a crowd which gathers to see what the catch was. One can hear the chaffing and bargaining going on by the side of the lake; one sees life and movement and action.

Thus is symbolized the kind of a religious man Jesus desires his preachers and pastors to be. He points away from the idea of solitariness of which the Eastern religions make so much. Had that been the idea of his ministry, he would have chosen shepherds in their loneliness beneath the sky and the stars. But he chose men who were in the thick of things. The ideal minister of Jesus Christ is not the monk, the friar, the Trappist, the conventual, the man shut off from the world; but rather the man in the world, though not of it, who shares the life, the interests, and activities of his fellows.

Another and even more evident reason for Jesus' choice of fishermen is that by their occupation they illustrated precisely the work which, as his disciples, they were to perform. This he made clear when, summoning them from their nets to follow him, he said to Simon: "Fear not; from henceforth thou shalt catch men." The word "catch" hardly gives the sense. In the margin of the Revised Version the Greek word is rendered "take alive." It is used only once again in the New Testament, in II Timothy 2:26: "That they may recover themselves out of the snare of the devil, who are taken captive by [God] at his will": as active instruments, that is, of his will. Such is to be the mission of Christ's appointed apostles: they were to take men alive for God. Thus the answer is implied to the sneering comment of the Apostate Julian: that Christ aptly termed his apostles fishermen: "for as the fisherman draws out the fish from the water to an element in which they cannot breathe but must presently perish, so these are to take men out of a world where they are free and happy into an existence that is both unnatural and unreal." Precisely the opposite is the teaching of Jesus. His apostles are to fish for men and lift them to a realm that is so surcharged with the energies of God that all of their native capacities will find their completion and fulfillment.

Thus the mission of Christ's apostle finds its perfect illustration in the business of fishing. In all that he says or does he is angling, trying to take a man alive for God. He has the fisherman's instinct, the fisherman's passion; he acquires the fisherman's skill. Always he is looking for opportunities to catch someone. He goes out after the careless, the indifferent, the drifting, the doubting, the sinning; goes out into the great teeming sea of life. Day by day, year after year he fishes for those who not yet have been captured unto the will of God. It is an interesting, absorbing, adventurous, romantic occupation. For, as happens to the fisherman, he often makes a catch where he least anticipates it and has the same joyful surprise.

Jesus taught his apostles how to fish for men. They must have watched him as he threw out his net day by day. Indeed, as we survey the Gospel record, no aspect of it is more familiar than this. He taught the people. He spoke his parables and told men of the kingdom of heaven. Yet clearly that was not his only occupation. He seems to have spent much of his time seeking to capture men unto the will of God. One after another he continued to draw them unto himself. His fishermen disciples were not slow to learn this lesson. They must have noted and sought to imitate his delicate skill and themselves become fishers of men. Thus from the beginning this became the divine method for saving the world.

The record of apostolic work as we find it in the New Testament shows the constant use of the fisherman's art. The apostles were preachers, but they never forgot that also they must catch men. Thus Philip the Evangelist fished for and caught the Ethiopian, and Peter the centurion. And what an expert fisherman was the Apostle Paul! His epistles are filled with the names of men and women whom he drew individually into the net he so skilfully cast — the names of high and low: Timothy, Titus, and Luke; Philemon the patrician; and Onesimus the runaway slave. One cannot read the record of his work without perceiving that he was constantly using every opportunity to capture men alive, one by one, by the personal method unto the will of God. So deeply embedded is the art of fishing for men in apostolic work and practice. And today the title of Fisherman is unofficially used by the Popes of Rome in commemoration of their descent from the fisherman Peter; and the "annulus piscatoris" is the special papal ring which is used to seal great documents. Every Pope has a new one made at his election. And every true minister of Jesus Christ should also have the title of Fisherman and wear the invisible fisherman's ring as a sign of his true apostleship.

Thus is set forth a peculiar aspect of the work of the parish minister. It is distinct from the work of general parish visitation in which he seeks to bring friendly aid and comfort to all of his parishioners. It is distinct also from his work as personal counselor in which he seeks to help men and women to solve critical problems in their experience. This is a specialized effort to persuade men to surrender their lives to God by the help of Jesus Christ and to commit themselves openly to Christian discipleship and to become communicant members of the Church. It is the work of personal evangelism — one of the most important and, one is sometimes tempted to believe, the least consecutively and seriously performed of all the tasks of the parish minister.

Evangelism has always been a central passion in a truly spiritual church, which seeks to bring to men outside of the Christian community the saving message of the Gospel. It has seemed terrible to its imagination that incalculable multitudes live unreached and untouched by the bodily and spiritual salvation which Christ is able to bring to them. It is piteous that everywhere are human beings without God or hope in the world, in whom are buried potentialities of divine communion. What is wanted is power

— dynamic force to cope with the mystery of existence, to bring men to a better state of living, to lift them and make them morally new. Hence the passion to reach men with the good news of the gospel and to transmit to them the power through Christ to become the sons of God. When the Church loses its evangelistic zeal it degenerates and ceases to be the Christ of God to society and forfeits its right to be called by his name.

The Madras Conference laid special emphasis upon the decline of the spirit of evangelism in the modern church. "The Church," it declared, "must always be moving; not to go forward is to regress. It dare not retreat. Its mission is to evangelize the world." [1] Yet the passion to evangelize the world is precisely what is most notably absent in many a church and, if the truth were told, in the heart of many a parish minister. He simply does not know how to go about it. Hence the practice of bringing in evangelists from outside the ranks of the local ministry to conduct evangelistic or revival campaigns of spiritual fervor and emotional appeal. These have their value. They do stir communities for the time being. They do win men to Christ. They do offer to parish ministers the opportunity of reaching and permanently attaching to the Church those who have been impressed by the message of the evangelist. Yet it is safe to say that the true evangelistic mission of the Church can be performed only as each church is the center of a true evangelism, as each minister is his own evangelist.

How then shall he give himself to the work as an evangelist? Without doubt, in the first place, by recovering

[1] *Report of Madras Conference*, pp. 28–29.

the habit of evangelistic preaching. Many a parish minister has lost the habit, the art, the ability to preach what are known as gospel sermons. It has been affirmed that "much of our preaching in the Church today would not be recognized as such by early Christians. It is teaching, exhortation or informal discussions of various aspects of our Christian life and thought addressed to congregations already established in the faith." [2] But it is not a heralding of the good news of salvation to men who are strangers to the Christian inspiration. And such "heralding" is what Christian preaching essentially is. It has even been questioned if instructional sermonizing is really preaching at all. It is teaching, and this has its place and its importance. But the distinction lies here: that whereas teaching is about a subject, preaching is directed toward a human object.

"It is easy," as Dr. Kerr says, "to preach on a variety of themes reflecting what is current in the news of the world, but only a disciplined mind and a consecrated heart can tell the 'old, old story' with effectiveness and evangelistic emphasis. But this must be done if the gospel is to be proclaimed." Men must be aroused to a sense of their need of God. Therefore every parish minister may well ask himself: How capable am I of preaching this type of sermon; how many sermons of mine hold this valid appeal to men to surrender themselves to Christ, who alone can bring eternal life?

The evangelistic work of the parish minister, however,

[2] C. H. Dodd, *The Apostolic Preaching and Its Development.* Quoted by Hugh Thompson Kerr in "Evangelism in Our Day," *Christendom*, Spring Issue, 1943.

does not end with the recovery of a truly evangelistic preaching. Indeed the chief value of this lies in the fact that when such warm and fructifying preaching has been done, the fishing is likely to be good. Occasionally after such preaching, it is true, some will present themselves to the minister and ask: "What must we do to be saved?" Yet this may not happen often. It may even surprise the minister when it does happen. Without doubt, it ought to happen oftener. But the minister is ill-advised if he waits for it and, if it does not occur, infer that his hearers are insensible to the appeal of the gospel. Rather he should allow for the reserves, the hesitancies, the reticences which keep them from responding of their own initiative to the impulse which has been inwardly felt. But now is the time for the minister to go fishing. Let him approach those whose hearts he has sought to stir by the gospel message and he will find many who gladly and even eagerly welcome the opportunity which he thus gives them to "accept Christ" and become members of his Church. Only a personal and pastoral evangelism will add "to the Church daily such as should be saved."

Too often the method of personal evangelism is confined by the minister to the children and youth of the church. These he gathers into classes and trains and prepares them for church membership. The work is congenial and presents no difficulties. And it has its great importance. But the same minister who is earnest and zealous in this work for the young shrinks from the duty of performing it for the adults in his church. He is sensitive about intruding into the religious life of men and women. He fears lest his motives may be misunderstood and his approach resented. He lacks the faith and courage to go to men with his straight appeal. Yet if he could but see beneath the surface, he would discover that it is quite otherwise; that these very people may actually be looking for him, hoping that he may come to them, while admitting that they could and even should go to him. Sometimes they may wonder why he does not come. "Oh, I knew that you would speak to me about this some day," said a woman to her minister when he went fishing for her. When he left her, he said to himself: "Suppose that I had not gone?" Never will any thoughtful man or woman resent such a visit.

A minister may walk into a man's business office, as more than one minister has done, and tell him why he has come, and by that simple act of faith capture a man alive for God. He has something of supreme value to offer, and he is not ashamed of the gospel. And the man to whom he has gone knows that he supremely needs what his minister has come to offer whether he accepts it or not. A minister once went fishing for a man in his congregation. "What is your business?" he asked. "I am a traveling salesman," was the reply. "So am I," said the minister, "and I know my business. First of all, I seek a personal interview. Next, I believe everlastingly in the goods I have to sell. Finally, I do not leave my prospect without a decision." "You do know your business," said the salesman. And there was a decision. The man's mother traveled three hundred miles to witness her son make his Christian confession on Easter day.

Only that type of pastoral evangelism can recruit the membership of the Church and give its preaching penetrating power. Some time ago the unchallenged statement was made that not ten churches of any denomination in one of our states could count ten men or women added to the church in three years from the non-Christian community. A lamentable number of churches show no increase whatever from year to year in their adult membership, except by transfer from other churches. The evangelistic passion is absent, evangelistic preaching has waned, and pastoral evangelism is unknown. Without doubt the laity should be instructed that fishing for men is their privilege also. No man really knows the essential joy of the Christian experience until he has helped some other man to be a Christian also. When anyone becomes a church member, he should be instructed that one of his most sacred duties is to try to bring another to the altar rail. If every disciple of Jesus Christ should understand that he must henceforth be a fisher for men, the Church would increase by leaps and bounds and the word of God would be magnified. The minister will teach his disciples, as Jesus did, how to fish. And in season and out of season he himself will be casting out his net for the souls of men.

Then there are the special seasons. The forty days of Lent may well be set aside by every earnest parish minister as a season of evangelistic preaching and personal evangelism. He will go carefully over his parish lists, noting the names of any who are not communicant members of the church. All during the parish year he will carefully preserve the names of those who in casual conversation, in informal ways, may have revealed themselves as open to persuasion and appeal. Then, in the pre-Lenten season, he will go fishing steadily day by day, omitting no one, however unlikely it may seem that he will respond. For in this romantic work of fishing one has constant, even unbelievable surprises. Laymen may and should assist in this Lenten work of parish evangelization, but the minister himself should always take the lead. The people are his, the sheep of his pasture, and he will personally seek to lead them to fountains of living waters. They will be asked to enroll themselves in a Lenten class to be held one evening during Lent for instruction in the meaning of church membership. Only rarely will anyone decline on the plea of lack of time. Of course if one is unable to attend, he may still make his confession of Christ with the others. But if this work is done with faithfulness, the minister will find himself each year with a sizeable group of adults all in earnest to listen and be taught the meaning of Christian discipleship.

It is best that membership in this special group be limited to those definitely preparing to unite with the Church. This class has its own restricted meaning and is not for the general instruction of others who may already be church members. A few, it may be, but only a few, when the six meetings are over, will feel that they are not ready to make their Christian confession. And no urgence will be applied. There will be respect for every man's conscience. Yet the rewards of such pastoral evangelism will be rich and ample.

Only in this way will the minister have done his full

Christian duty. Here also he will discover his deepest
Christian joy. The absence of joy in the parish ministry
is due, perhaps more than to anything else, to the fact that
the minister does not more often know the spiritual happiness of having seen another to whom he has sought to
bring the Word of Life find his way into the kingdom of
heaven. Nothing will so redeem what often appears to be
the tedium and routine of the minister's lot like these
flashes of romanticism, of spiritual illumination in the
human soul. He never recovers from the miracle of it,
the beauty of it, the unending joy of it.

When Bishop Charles H. Slattery was in the Episcopal
Theological School at Cambridge, he had a mission parish.
One Lent he formed his confirmation class, of which every
member except one was duly confirmed. When Dr. Slattery returned to Massachusetts as Bishop, he revisited the
mission church. Alone, he found himself in the room
where that class had been held and was thinking of it
when he realized that someone else had entered. "You do
not remember me," said the man, "but I am the only member of the confirmation class you held here so many years
ago who was not confirmed." Quick as a flash, and with
true fisherman's instinct, the Bishop threw out his net.
"But it is not too late," he said. And one more life was
captured unto the will of God.

CHAPTER 10

Give Good Gifts to Your Children

THE minister who is not fond of children, does not understand them, or is not interested in them, is to this extent disqualified to be a parish minister. For the children are not only the Church of the future, they are the citizens-to-be by whom our new world must be built. And the minister who loves his girls and boys may exercise a profound and permanent influence on their characters. He has no more sacred task than to give good gifts to his children.

Our age has been extraordinarily interested in childhood. Medical science has made great progress in the study and prevention of children's diseases. Social science has devoted its attention to child welfare, from milk stations and day nurseries to playgrounds and libraries. Pedagogy has been tremendously interested in the child and has sought to determine the best principles of mental development and training. Thus it has become inevitable that increased attention should be given to the child's moral and religious education. We have produced a generation of children who have healthy bodies and well-trained minds, but many of whom do not know the meaning of morals or possess real religion as a controlling force in life and conduct.

Yet never did children and youth need morals and religion more than they do today. The safety of our sons and daughters as they go out into the world day by day depends upon the adequacy of their religious education. Moral pitfalls in the way of growing children are now far more numerous than they have ever been. Boys and girls have innumerable opportunities for going wrong. Child delinquency has become one of our gravest problems and the lawlessness of American youth has become a by-word. At no time in our history has the moral and religious training of children been so necessary. Not only their safety, but that of our whole social order depends directly upon it. Hence church leaders, educators, social workers have been facing this problem and seeking to solve it. The attempt to introduce more of explicit religious instruction in our public schools has not succeeded and there is no reason to believe that it will and can succeed. The effort to have week-day religious instruction given by the churches either singly or in groups to children who are excused from the public schools for the purpose has made some progress. But as things are now the difficulties are so great that large results from this approach to the problem can hardly be expected. We are, therefore, so far as Protestantism is concerned, thrown back upon the home and upon the Sunday teaching of the Church as the only reliable sources of moral and religious training.

Home influence at its best is without doubt the deepest and most determining form of religious education that a child can receive. This influence is subtle, constant, and pervading. The ideals of godly parents become insensibly the ideals of their children. Family tradition and standards of honor are held sacred by them. As one of them said when urged to a certain course of conduct by a sophisticated friend: "That kind of thing isn't done in our family." Religion, too, at its purest and best is learned in the home. The boy or girl sees, knows, recognizes it as the real thing exemplified in the character of mother and father. Whatever else may be right or wrong, true or false, to live as these lived and to believe what made them as they are, must be right and true. Religion is still best learned at one's mother's knee.

Thus, if all homes could be religious and Christian homes, if the child from his birth hour could be taught as he grows up in his home to know the meaning and value of Bible, of prayer, of the teaching and worship of the Church, the problem if not solved would be vastly less critical than it is. We have to reckon, however, with the fact that modern conditions of living have greatly altered the character of the average American home. Family prayers have all but disappeared. Even grace before meals is the exception. Things are different today from what they were a generation ago. Influences are at work which disrupt family life, week days and Sundays alike. Life for the children has become socially far more complicated. No longer does the family gather quietly together in the evening. All kinds of excitements lure the children elsewhere. Two automobiles have become a necessity for a family of any size in order that its members may travel in opposite directions at the same time. Sunday habits have changed. It is difficult today to maintain family life at its best.

Again we have to reckon with a high degree of parental irresponsibility so far as religious education is concerned. Carefully trained in all other respects, children are often allowed to grow up religiously as they please. Many parents who are made anxious by adenoids and measles are apparently not concerned that the love and fear of God be planted in a child's heart. Parents who devote hours to getting their children into the right secular schools and into the hands of good teachers do not take the same interest in their religious instruction. If they send their children to church school, it never occurs to them to visit the school, to cooperate with the teacher, to interest themselves in what their children are studying, or to help them in the learning of their Bible lessons. And by their own absenteeism from church they let their children understand how little they value what the Church has to offer. "You don't realize," said a mother to the minister who had called to inquire why her daughter was no longer attending church school, "how much children have to do nowadays. Elizabeth just had to drop something."

It is no wonder if children coming from such homes never learn what real religion is or how it operates to control moral behavior.[1] Such parents often are bewildered at the way their children behave after they leave home and begin to live on their own. Why should their son who was such a good, meek lad at home and whose school marks were so good, behave like the devil when he got to college? As a matter of fact there is no mystery at all. A child may be good because he has no chance to go wrong. He lives in the unfailing presence of nurses, parents, teachers. He hardly knows a moment when he is free to do as he pleases. And he never was trained to stand on his own

[1] See George Hodges, *The Training of Children in Religion.* D. Appleton and Company, 1911.

moral legs. There was never constructed within him that self-operating bit of moral machinery whose motive power is religion. He was accustomed to be good, but he did not of his own choice and desire want to be good. And no child is safe unless he himself wants to be good and has the self-control which will enable him to be good. Religious education is training a child to act from religious motives. And the home is where this training most consistently should be given. The ultimate solution of the problem of religious education lies in the reformation of the American home. As Ruskin has said, the history of a nation is not the history of its wars, but of its households.

Under these circumstances, the religious training of children in the church becomes a matter of major importance, because for many, if not for the majority, this is the only explicit religious instruction they receive. And the inadequacy of the instruction which reaches Protestant children in their churches is a matter of common knowledge. Jewish children receive every year 335 hours of religious teaching; Roman Catholic children, 200 hours a year. And Protestant children average less than 30 hours a year. Protestant church schools are given scant financial support by their churches, which will spend $1.46 annually per member for their music, $1.07 for janitor service, and $.48 for its church school; they get results in proportion. The teachers are for the most part unpaid and pedagogically untrained. The attendance of pupils is voluntary and often irregular. The curriculum is a matter of constant discussion and frequent change. What can best be taught? How can it be made to interest the children? How can the subject matter be so integrated as to leave a definite and constructive deposit of knowledge of the Bible, the salient facts of the Christian beliefs of the Church, its history, its cultus in the minds of children and youth? All of this is an unsolved and often it appears an unsolvable problem. One thing only is sure. The instruction should be thoroughly biblical, with a definitely Christian basis and content.

Thus there is presented to the parish minister an important, difficult, but absorbingly interesting sphere of activity. If he is wise, he will not be discouraged nor will he be in any defeatist mood. It is easy to rail at our church schools. No one has any difficulty at all in picking flaws in them, in finding fault with them, in contrasting the discipline, regularity and for the most part competent teaching in our day schools with what one finds in the churches. It requires more insight, more knowledge, more experience to discover the enormous amount of good being accomplished by the average church school even under conditions that have been described. Taken just as it is, it represents a positive and indispensable influence in the religious training of our children and youth. If parents, instead of criticizing, would helpfully cooperate, that influence would be vastly increased. If churches could be farsighted enough to give it adequate financial support, much more could be done. But as he finds it, the whole field of the religious training of the children and youth of the church offers an alluring opportunity to the parish minister. He should survey it as a whole, direct it according to well-defined principles, and recognize the range and depth of his own personal influence on the lives of his church children.

He will, then, begin with the parents and try to obtain their closer and more intimate knowledge of what is going on in the church school and seek their cooperation. Frequent announcements will be made to the congregation and reports of church-school activities will be printed on the church bulletin. Parents will be invited to special assemblies of the school and to demonstrations of the work that is being done, and parents' meetings will be held. This work, kept up year after year, will bring results where most needed.

The minister will keep in close touch with the teachers in all departments of the school, plan their work with them, attend and address teachers' meetings. After all that is said about the ineffectiveness of the average Sunday-school teacher, there is no more devoted or helpful or influential group of people in the service of the Church than those who, week after week, are doing their work under severe handicaps in the religious teaching of the children. They may not be trained in some ways, but they are in others. Dean Hodges once said, in commenting on the habit of bringing in paid teachers from outside the parish into our church schools, that he would rather have a child meet week after week with a devoted Christian man or woman who lacked pedagogical training, than to have him given the best technical teaching by one who lacked the inward experience of real religion. Children in the long run have their characters formed by subtle and invisible influences and one of the most potent of these is the transmission of grace through a consecrated personality. On the walls of a certain parish house hung, years ago, a banner with stars indicating the banner class for the year. Many times over was inscribed "Miss Edwards' class." One tries in vain to estimate the value of that consecrated life on the hundreds of girls who came under her influence.

We are told that the day of the Sunday school is over, that new methods must be devised for the religious training of children. Without doubt many of these are desirable and the minister must always keep abreast of new trends and be constantly adapting his work to them. He ought, however, never to undervalue the religious influence of the group-teacher. The chances are strong that if our schools, as they are at present organized, do their best work, the child before he graduates will have a fair knowledge of the Bible and will have learned what the Christian religion is. As things are today, seventy-five per cent of the children in our church schools become church members before they leave them. And the majority of these become dependable church-goers and workers.

Ministers will allow their children to grow up of themselves until they become of high-school age. He will visit frequently the primary and junior departments and talk to the boys and girls who thus come to know him, feel intimate with him, and understand his interest in and affection for them. He will also roam through the school as a whole and occasionally teach a group in the absence of the teacher. He will be present at assembly hours, at the periods of worship, and talk to the whole school frequently. He may have the habit of preaching brief children's sermons to the younger members of the school who attend the first part of the morning service of the church. In all of these ways an intimacy develops between the minister and the children which lies at the basis of all of his influence on their lives.

When, however, the children grow into adolescence, a new series of problems presents itself. Then the minister must come to know them individually. The youth require special attention. They may have outgrown the class method of teaching and require organizations of their own both on Sundays and between Sundays. The forum method or the youth fellowship method now comes into being and these require special pastoral attention and guidance. Intimately the minister associates himself with these groups and directly, though subtly, his influence must be felt on each separate life. On the occasion celebrating the twenty-fifth anniversary of his appointment as Abbot professor of theology at Andover Seminary, Daniel Evans is reported to have said: "I consider it my function to lead, not control; to inspire, not to dominate; to emancipate, not to subjugate." No better words could be found to define the kind of influence which the wise parish minister will seek to exert upon the youth of the church as they come to face the many moral problems which confront them. He will not argue or urge or seek to control. He will love them, trust them, believe in them. He will speak simply of his own faith, his own standards, his own convictions. Above all he will hold up before them the example of his own healthy, fortified, consecrated life. In these ways, he will do for the youth of his church beyond his imagining. A mother once said that her son had told her that what he desired above everything was to merit the good opinion of the man who was his minister and had helped to bring him up from babyhood. Such is the reward of every true minister who seeks to give good gifts to his children.

Sometimes the work of the teacher is contrasted with that of the preacher. Education, we are told, "is a far more powerful agent than preaching, inasmuch as in the first place it acts upon the human being at an age where he is more susceptible to moral influences than he afterwards becomes; and in the second place it acts upon him incessantly, intensely, over a series of years, whereas preaching acts upon him intermittently and by one uniform method. There is no moral influence in the world, excepting that occasionally exerted by great men, comparable to that of a good teacher; there is no position in which a man's merits considered as moral levers have so much purchase." The great privilege of the parish minister, however, lies in the fact that for him this contrast does not exist, for he is both preacher and teacher at the same time. His is not the intermittent and uniform influence of the preacher only; he possesses also the opportunity of bringing his personality to bear "incessantly and intensely" upon the lives of children and youth at their most susceptible age.

At high-school age comes one of the most critical moments in their religious development, the act of decision by which they who have learned about Christ now declare themselves to be for Christ and become henceforth and forever members of the Society of the Friends of Jesus which is the Church. At this moment, the minister himself becomes their teacher. They who have hitherto been taught the rudiments of Christian knowledge by others shall now be taught by him what is their obligation and privilege to become corporate members of the Church universal.

For the church school is a preparatory school. Just as secular preparatory schools fit their pupils for college, so the church school prepares its pupils for church. They will graduate from the church school as they do from the day school. But before they graduate they must form their attachment to the Church, into the life of which they will enter when they leave the school. The school is not a substitute for the Church. It does not bring the child into accord with the ancient and valuable and universal expression of corporate devotion. It does not initiate him into that Society in which he should have his membership all the rest of his life. Therefore the minister must see by his own special training that the transition is made by his children with full understanding of its importance and meaning. If he can succeed in helping them to link their lives with the life of Christ and with his Body which is the Church, he has then given them his best and highest gift.

Except in Episcopal churches, when the time for confirmation classes is arranged according to the annual visitation of the bishop, these instruction classes are usually held during Lent and their members are received into the church at the Easter season. During the pre-Lenten period, therefore, the parish minister will carefully draw up a list of those eligible by age to his class, which will be held each week on a certain day and at a stated hour known to every girl and boy. He will talk to the school about it on several Sundays before its meetings begin, explaining its purpose and methods; he will hold a parents' meeting enlisting their cooperation; he will speak to the teachers, asking them to tell their groups what church membership has meant to them; he will be careful to see personally those boys and girls who he feels may need a special invitation or word of encouragement. Indeed, he will neglect nothing that may aid to the formation of as large and thoughtful a group as is possible. But he will urge none. Their interest and attendance must be of their own choice and desire. When the group first meets, he will tell them frankly that if any have come not of their own free will, they should not come again, and that he will not follow up any who drop out because this will show that they are not really interested. As a result of this technique, he is likely to receive such notes as these: "I am sorry that I was unable to come to class this afternoon. I was in bed with a cold." "I am sorry that I forgot class last week. However I am planning to come regularly from now on." He will have a surprisingly regular and wholly voluntary attendance of the great majority.

The instruction will cover the whole area of subjects necessary to an intelligent understanding of what the Church is — its fundamental beliefs; the meaning and importance of the sacraments; the meaning of Christian discipleship; the duties and privileges of church membership; the importance of religious habits of Bible-reading, of prayer, of faithful church attendance, of regular offerings, of setting a good example to others. The form of instruction will differ according to the minister's own ideas. The catechetical method is not often used, but it has its distinct advantages, and the putting of a little book or pamphlet or catechism into the hands of each to serve as a guide always increases attention. The talks by the minister will be human, full of anecdotal and illustrative material, and always interesting. Questions and answers will break up any formality and uniformity. And there will be plenty of humor interspersed throughout. Nothing that a minister does is more fascinating than to conduct such a class as this. Outsiders, even parents and teachers, will not be admitted. He will have the children to himself and he can make a profound impression upon them. The decisions in each case will be personal and again without any urging by the minister. Some members of the class in a given year may not become members of the Church. But those who do will know what it means and why they are doing it.

When it is all over, the minister will receive some more letters: "This is just a little note of thanks for your showing me the right path of life. I got from class a whole new slant. No one will ever know how much church membership means to me and I do hope that I will be called a true follower of Christ;" "You have rendered me invaluable help this year in class. You have changed my whole attitude toward the church. Now I go to it out of pure desire;" "I have decided to have my first Holy Communion at Easter;" "I want to tell you how I have enjoyed your classes. They have made things clearer about Jesus Christ and the Church. I know that I will never regret the step I am taking;" "The class will never be forgotten by any of us who were in it. Then things first began to take hold and have real meaning: from the vivid worth-while stories to the deep complex problems." Thus the minister, to his own deepest delight, finds that he has indeed given good gifts to his children.

The Church has its own recipe for the creation of character. Educators tell us that the only way to train a child religiously and morally is to hold up before him someone whom he admires and desires to be like. Boys and girls are naturally hero-worshipers. In imitation of the one whom they admire, all their motives and impulses will fall into line as they seek to grow into the likeness of their hero. The Church very simply holds up the person of Christ, in loyalty to whom one will be set down among princes and inherit a crown of glory. Does the Church's recipe work? Does it actually create character? Some years ago Judge Lewis L. Fawcett of Brooklyn made the astonishing statement that of 4000 boys less than twenty-one years of age arraigned before him during eighteen years that he had sat on the bench in two courts, only three were members of a Sunday school at the time of the commission of their crimes, and that these three were guilty of only technical misdemeanors. On the basis of this experience, he did not hesitate to declare that regular attendance at Sunday school during adolescence is signally preventive against crime and exerts a powerful influence on character formation.[2] Despite all difficulties, all shortcomings, the Church is doing a powerful work of religious education. It is bringing up a generation of children and youth of which it has a right to be proud.

The parish minister does no more beautiful and romantic work than to bring his influence to bear in skilful human, constant ways upon the lives of his children. To know them, to love them; to know that he has their affection and loyalty; to be able to guide them as they grow from childhood to youth, and from youth to manhood and womanhood; to have them come to him with their problems; to give counsel and direction to them; to watch them as they grow into Christian character and usefulness, all of this is perhaps one of the deepest satisfactions of his ministry. No minister ever loses his reward who seeks day by day, in season and out of season, by every method that love and understanding can supply, to give good gifts to his children.

[2] As reported in *The Literary Digest* for January 31, 1925.

CHAPTER 11

In the Beauty of Holiness

✤ ✤ ✤ ✤ ✤ ✤ ✤

PERHAPS nothing in the world is more beautiful and mystical than the love of the soul for the sanctuary. How impressive are these shrines of the spirit uplifted by the delicate, God-lonesome soul of man; "frozen music" as Goethe once called them, in which men have sought to embody and make eloquent the hidden voiceless presence which hallows the earth. Some deep necessity in man draws heavy stones and timbers together like a magnet and builds them into a home of the soul, its altars firesides of prayer, its spires incarnations of aspiration. Their steps are worn by the feet of men and women who foregather there and turn their faces, seamed with care and wet with weeping, toward the far-off city of God. These places of worship, whether they be cathedrals or the humble houses of God that one finds wherever men live together, are loved because they are saturated with the prayers of many generations and are filled with the most sacred memories. To many they are the holiest spots on earth. They are full of the beauty of holiness.

Thither the tribes of Israel still go up. The number of people who retain the habit of church-going and the regularity with which they practice it depends upon the invisible and incalculable fluctuations of the spirit, both in the outer world and in the inward experience of the individual. But the instinct is there. Let one watch a company of people, young and old, making their way into the house of God, and ask himself: What brings them there; what keeps bringing them there? There is *au fond* but one answer: the sanctuary is the trysting-place between the soul and God where, in company with one's fellow pilgrims, one looks for the viaticum, the spiritual provision for life's journey. "The assembling of people who are bent on prayer is something singularly beautiful. There are here a nobleness and an elevation of soul which have no counterpart in any other gathering in the world." The soul is here in the presence of the Eternal. "This is none other but the house of God, and this is the gate of heaven." On the wings of angels the burden of the human heart is borne upward to the throne of God.

Above and beyond all else, then, the Church makes provision for the worshiping instinct of the human heart. Throughout all human history this has been the central meaning of the sanctuary. Thus the Church, to do its real work in the modern world, must minister to the hearts of men by communicating to them the very life of God, by satisfying the human longing for a vision of God that shall bring them peace and power and joy. It must organize itself in the beauty of holiness as a channel for the transmission of divine grace. It must not rely solely on public exhortation. The chief end of any service which calls itself religious is to create the sense of the presence of God; to withdraw the human spirit from things visible to things invisible and thus, for a time at least, make the spiritual world more real than the sensible world.

Thus the deepest need is a revival of the attitude of awe and wonder in worship. Many congregations today present the aspect of spectators or auditors, and are frequently called "audiences." Yet the central element in religion has always been mystery, and worship is the contemplation of that mystery and the feeling of awe which is thus evoked in the worshiper. In the celebration of the Roman Catholic mass, the worshiper contemplates the word of God made flesh and offered him in the mass. "Here is something, he feels, that lies beyond reason, dimly seen through sacred symbols, but not to be logically explained. And the power of this appeal is witnessed by the fact that to millions of Christians this is the living core of their religion. They submit themselves to the charm of mystery which draws them out of a world of fact into a world of faith." [1]

In the Protestant Church, this central mystery is the gospel. Paul often calls it just that. And this mystery is something that essentially is not to be rationalized, but to be felt and so accepted as bringing salvation. Hence the elevation of the gospel even as the priest elevates the Host becomes the most sacred duty of the Christian minister. It is not something to be debated and argued about, although it has its basis in reason and can be justified by reason. Too often Protestantism has sought to make this mystery rational, logical, intellectually comprehensible, and thus has taken the heart out of it. For essentially religion is not what can be comprehended; it is reverence for the incomprehensible. It is not that which can be grasped and compassed by the reason alone; it is awe for what is beyond reason. It is not something which can be deduced by logic; it is wonder before the illogical or

[1] See article "The Vanishing Art of Worship" by William J. Dawson, *Century Magazine*, September, 1923.

the alogical. It is bewilderment and surprise at the vision which is spread before men, but which is not arrived at by them. T. R. Glover has said that Christianity conquered paganism because the early Christians "out-thought, out-lived, and out-died the pagans." It would not have won this victory had it only "out-thought" paganism. What enabled the early Christians to out-live and out-die the pagans was precisely the possession of the central "mysterium" which is the gospel. It is a reality which may seem foolishness to the secular mind but which to the believer is salvation itself.

This truth has its supreme illustration in the sacraments. Yet every church service should have a sacramental character and significance. It must be the minister's supreme aim to see that the service of worship is invested with the garment of beauty and makes its appeal to the wondering instincts of the human heart. We need the recovery of the mystical temper in both preacher and people. Intellectualism will always have its place. The appeal to the emotions is always valid. But the things of God are most truly revealed to the pure of heart who immediately feel them, see them, and so know them to be true. Here lies the justification for symbolism in religion: of "the outward and visible signs of the inward and spiritual grace" on which the eye can rest until the reality for which they stand somehow penetrates the soul.[2] It is by the vision of something that astonishes us that the soul

[2] The reader is referred to *Christian Symbolism in the Evangelical Churches* by Thomas R. Stafford, 1942, for a helpful discussion of this subject.

137

expands. It is by the apprehension of a reality which awes and humbles us that we become truly and deeply religious men and women.

Thus the highest and most delicate task of the parish minister lies in his function as leader of his people in the act of worship. Here he is exercising the highest function of human life, for what higher task can be offered any man than to assist his fellow men to pass beyond the horizon of the visible and the temporal and to see "the king in his beauty in the land that is very far off." Ministers in our day are being prepared for everything else they have to do. But all too often they have not been adequately prepared for this, the most difficult of all their tasks; and all too often also they have not themselves realized the importance, the meaning, the infinite significance of it. As a result, the element of worship has been so neglected in many churches, that the question has been asked: "Do Protestants Worship?" [8] To the recovery of this central function of the church, and to the training of ministers in the exercise of it, much attention has lately been paid by church leaders. And none too soon. For the church which has ceased to be a center of worship has lost its authority and influence over the lives of men.

The minister will approach in the spirit of deepest reverence the hour of worship when he is to stand before the people and seek to lead them to the very threshold of eternal realities. Here are men, women, and children in every variety of human need — in the deepest need of all

[8] Article in *The Christian Century* by John Clarence Petie, July 30, 1941.

if they are unconscious of their need. And here is the place of prayer, the altar, the visible symbols of the presence of God. Here is the possibility that a spark of the divine life shall be communicated to some human soul; that some immediate awareness of God shall be granted it; that some sense of God shall be felt; that the reality of things unseen shall, if only for the moment, be grasped and known. Surely such an hour is filled with spiritual romance. If worshipers when they leave the house of God have risen to "the positive experience of the real presence of God and [been] bathed with the joy of that experience," the Church has fulfilled its function.

The minister who is sensitive to the spiritual romance of every hour of worship is superior to numbers. The fact of a worshiping congregation is what impresses him, not the size of it. For always there are romantic possibilities in the smallest assembly. From this point of view, one understands where lay the sin of David in numbering the people. A fundamental irreverence in Protestantism is measuring the "success" of a church service by the number of worshipers. Numbers do not tell the story at all. Sometimes one goes into a church which is crowded to the doors and comes away with the disheartening sense that one has not been at church at all. At other times, one goes into a church where there have been only a handful of worshipers and feels that one has been in the very presence of the Eternal.

A parish minister once went in Florence to an afternoon service in the Church of Santa Croce, one of the most beautiful and one of the few Gothic churches in Italy.

Tourists were moving about. But the service began, with full choir and clergy. It was a service of incomparable beauty, an hour in length. The congregation consisted of six persons, two of whom were children. At length the white-robed procession of priests left the chancel. Little did they realize what they had done: the lesson they had taught a visiting Protestant minister that would last him all his days. Never since that day and hour has he been tempted to evaluate the significance of a church service from the number of attendants. When Bishop Westcott was Dean of Peterborough Cathedral, he went one very rainy Sunday afternoon to conduct the four o'clock service. There were present only the verger and one worshiper. On his return home, his daughter took off his wet cloak, put his slippers before the fire, and prepared tea. "Father," she said, "was anybody there?" "Full," he replied, "full of the glory of the Lord between Cherubim and Seraphim."

Let the parish minister put the accent on numbers and he will be tempted to use every kind of device to induce more people to come to church. There is a legitimate use of publicity in bringing to the attention of people what the church has to offer them.[4] There are also illegitimate and meretricious methods of advertising services which are beneath the Church's dignity. It is not the duty of any minister to see how many people he can persuade to come inside his church. His duty lies in striking the spiritual note and providing an hour of real worship when there have been put into active operation spiritual

---

[4] A helpful discussion of this subject is found in *How to Make Friends for Your Church* by John L. Fortson, Association Press, 1943.

forces that bear the test of being valid and serviceable aids to daily living. If one lame man has been made to walk, one leper has been cleansed, one blind man has been made to see, a sacramental work of immeasurable meaning has been performed. If men and women can go away with renewed strength to bear their burdens; if the hour of worship stirs within them new yearnings, new desires, fresh hopes and consecrated enthusiasms, then the Church at the moment and hour that it has done this thing has accomplished its purpose for humanity. And a truly spiritual church has nothing to fear. To it men at some moment of their experience, weary of seeking to cope with the mysteries of existence, will be sure to turn. Miracles of grace may happen at any hour of worship. The minister expects them to happen. Thus he comes up to every service of worship with the most glowing spiritual expectations. Surely nothing in life can be more romantic than this.

The minister in this delicate and beautiful task will seek to have the visible setting of the act of worship, the sanctuary, appeal to the imagination, to the aesthetic sense, the love of the beautiful. In our day there has been a healthy recovery from the Puritan distrust of beauty as a road to God.[5] And the beautifying of the sanctuary has this justification — that it immeasurably helps the soul of man in its effort to see, feel, and apprehend the fact and being of God. The aesthetic instinct is as deep and inalienable as the mind's love of truth and the soul's

[5] See Von Ogden Vogt, *Art and Religion,* 1921, and *Modern Worship,* 1927.

love of goodness. Thus every effort to beautify the church
and make it lovely to the eye and senses is reproducing in
its own way what has been the history-long instinct of
the human heart. Whatever can be done in loving devotion with regard to what is intrinsically beautiful of
itself, is woven from the same pattern of love as the best
that the mediaeval artists could achieve. And the purpose
is the same: to help the struggling human soul through
beauty to an immediate vision of God. We toil toward
God with our minds trying to construct an idea of God
out of the materials with which our thinking has to do;
we struggle up the hill of holiness with our wills trying
to achieve those moral victories through which we can
come to him. But there is this something else: a glimpse
and so a knowledge of God that comes when we see
beauty. When the worshiper enters a beautiful sanctuary,
his soul is inevitably lifted toward God. The need here is
that the minister should possess and use this sense of
beauty, that valid aid be brought to the God-seeking soul.

The church service will have its framework, its form and
order within which is enshrined the truth which it has
to offer men. In the so-called liturgical churches, this
form is fixed and uniform. Where a book of common
prayer is used and followed, ministers are usually instructed in its history and use. In the so-called non-
liturgical churches, each minister is free to arrange the
form of the service according to his own convictions —
all the more reason that he should be taught the spiritual
principles which underlie the progression of a true service
of worship. It is not a question of a given order of service,

but rather a grasp of the underlying ideas which in their true sequence will awaken and satisfy the worshiping instincts of the human heart. Thus the congregation will be led step by step from adoration to confession, thanksgiving, intercession, petition, and finally to the consecration of life anew to God. Literature in abundance now exists to guide the minister in the theory and practice of worship.[6] A proper framework within which the act of worship can most readily and naturally take place is an elemental necessity. For if it is true that form without spirit is dead, it is also true that under human conditions spirit without form cannot be apprehended. Form of itself cannot produce worship; rather it is the worshipful instinct which creates the form. Thus the only question worth discussing is: What is the proper form for the spirit of worship to wear?[7] The recovery of a true form of worship without any loss of a true spirit of worship is the end to be held in view.

For the conduct of each service the minister will make the most careful preparation. Often ministers toil over the sermon, but make quick work of getting ready for what, after all, is the most difficult part of his task: the service of worship. Aware of its deep meanings, one will spend much time over its every detail. It may take half an hour properly to select three hymns. He will remember that the reading of Scripture is really presenting to the

[6] The reader is referred to the October, 1942, Bulletin of the General Theological Library for a full bibliography on public worship compiled by Dean Willard L. Sperry and Rev. Henry Wilder Foote.

[7] This subject is fully discussed in the author's *The Christian Church in the Modern World*, Chapter VII, "The Worship of the Church."

143

congregation a Bible sermon of incomparable beauty, for all Bible writers were preachers. Lectionaries exist to aid him in the choice of what shall be read, and he will go over this again and again until it becomes a very part of him. The prayers present him alike with his greatest opportunity and gravest responsibility. For this office, only the severest spiritual discipline will suffice whether the prayers be read or whether they be free prayer. The preparation for this deepest service of all goes deep, far back of the occasion itself: its sources lie in the minister's personal and evangelical experience of God.[8]

True prayer is not the language of the school but of the heart. One who really aspires to lead the prayers of the people will thus train himself to the point of saturation with Bible language and with historic and individual forms of devotion. For in the oldest liturgies is found worship at high estate. But above all, he will keep rich and warm within himself the realities of the Christian experience of God which can touch, quicken, and illumine all the varied experiences and needs of men.

There must be unity in a service, of course, and this will be carefully studied. Yet it is a mistake to have but one idea run through the whole service, reiterated in Scripture, hymn, prayer, and sermon. There are diversities of need in the congregation that one idea cannot possibly meet. The subject of the sermon, let us say, is the dignity of labor. Thus the first hymn is Go Labor On, Spend and Be Spent. The Scripture lessons are from Proverbs: "Go to the ant thou sluggard," and from the Gospel: "The

[8] From the author's *The Eloquence of Christian Experience*, p. 206.

laborers in the vineyard." The hymn following the sermon is Work for the Night Is Coming. Here is unity of idea. But in the congregation is a poor woman whose whole week has been filled with back-breaking work. And she looks in vain for a word of comfort or of rest. Why should the Scripture bear on the sermon? Why should every hymn intone the same idea? The service of worship should contain varied ideas to suit an infinite variety of needs. Perhaps the finest test of a minister's sensitiveness, it has been said, is his ability to attain through all the instruments at his command a cumulative unity of impression, which is quite different from unity of idea.

The two moods integral to any service of worship are the contrasted moods of quietness and of joy. On the one hand there is stillness. The spirit of God has hard work to cast its spell upon a congregation which is engaged, up to the moment the service begins, in more or less noisy talk and interchange of greetings and remarks. For silence is the very secret and medium of spiritual efficacy. It is one of the most evident and indispensable conditions of real worship. The words, "Be still and know that I am God," might well be placed before the eyes of many a modern congregation. Of the spiritual possibilities of stillness, every one of us must have had some vivid experience. Thus nature best ministers to us. The Church needs to recapture this ministry of silence. The friendly noisiness and sibilant conversations appropriate enough at other times and places, when carried on as they are thoughtlessly in the moments preceding or following the service of worship, are the source of untold loss in the spiritual ministry possible to the Church in our modern world.

On the other hand, the jubilant note should penetrate the service and give lift and power to its spiritual message. The early church was a singing church and every victorious church of Christ has literally shouted for joy. A dumb congregation denies its faith. When the call to worship goes forth, the congregation will by its cooperative and joyful response produce a powerful spiritual impression. It ought to be impossible for anyone a stranger to the meaning of the evangel to come into a service of the Church without being made to feel, and to respond to, its dominant note: "This is the victory which overcometh the world, even our faith." The Psalmist understood this when he said: "Let the people praise thee, O God, let all the people praise thee: then God even our own God will bless us and all the ends of the earth shall fear him."

People also should be allowed a certain freedom in the matter of coming to church. The usual assumption is that they should be in their pews before the service begins and should not leave them until it ends — an etiquette too severe and formal. It is possible that some are not really strong enough to take the whole of the service. Others may not wish to, but would like to be present for part of it. They should be free to come and go as they please. The idea that a worshiper is guilty of an act of rudeness to the minister if he leaves the church during the hymn before the sermon should be dismissed at once. A church is not a lecture hall and the minister is not a public speaker. He should never allow himself to be disturbed either by late comers, or by those leaving the church during the service. People should look upon the church as their spiritual home, in which they feel this sense of freedom.

It is a mistake to exhort people to come on time or to print notices to that effect on the church bulletin. If this is done, some who really plan and want to come but have been detained will look at the clock and, remembering the exhortation, will stay at home. The continuous coming of worshipers after a service has begun has something beautiful about it from one point of view, and this should never be regarded as an interruption or disturbance. It were better that one should come, if only for the benediction, rather than not to come at all.

It is a pity that people should be shut out of the sanctuary for six days out of seven. It should be open every day to welcome any with burdens on their hearts who desire to enter for the purpose of silent prayer, meditation, and communion with God. We live in a troubled and noisy world. Opportunity should be given men to escape from it at any hour of the day and find quietness and peace in God's sanctuary. The sight of closed doors does not speak well for a church. Its doors should be open. Within it is to be found what cannot be found anywhere else and this should be made available to men at any time of need. Nothing is more touching than the sight of a single worshiper at prayer in the solitude of the sanctuary. Even if no one should enter, the open doors of the church would be its sign of welcome: "Whosoever will, let him come." The spiritual influence of a church in this way will make itself intangibly felt, and the importance of this is such that ways should be found to surmount any difficulties that may present themselves.

Beyond and beneath all that has been said is the personality, the spirit, the attitude of the minister himself. He must appear before the Lord and before his people in the beauty of holiness; hence anything which is careless in manner or demeanor, in word or in act is most studiously avoided. By no means is he to be stilted or inhuman. On the contrary, he will be full of vitality and human feeling. There may even be touches of humor. Yet everything that he is and does is of the very essence of reverence. Every community needs men who care for life in its proper poetry, what Cardinal Newman once called its "legitimate rhetoric." Men want artists whom they can trust when they come to church. They ought to come in confidence that no carelessness or ignorance, no violation of taste shall get between them and their desire to be led in acts of devotion. Only in the beauty of holiness lies the romance of worship.

CHAPTER 12

I Taught You Publicly

✠ ✠ ✠ ✠ ✠ ✠ ✠

WE know from this word of the Apostle Paul that preaching to a given Christian assembly, to a settled congregation of believers was a part of the Christian cultus from the very birth-hour of the Church. And ever since then, the sermon has had its place in the Christian service of worship. Only when the Church has lost its spiritual vigor and zeal has the sermon been neglected, minimized or forgotten. Preaching has always accompanied the mission of the Church to the world, given it wings and caused it to have penetrating power on the lives of men and on the life of the world. It has indeed a romantic tradition.

Sometimes the question is raised as to the comparative merits and importance of the service of worship as distinguished from the sermon itself. The antithesis is unfortunate. These are not separate and independent parts of the church service; rather they are component and mutually dependable elements of it. The worship prepares the congregation for the sermon, and the sermon itself is an act of worship in which the whole congregation has its share. In a pregnant passage in the Epistle to the Romans (15:16) Paul expressly defines preaching as worship.[1] Its style and phraseology have a certain sacerdotal form and character. Here is a priest at the altar making an oblation which is sanctified by the Holy Ghost. Preaching

[1] This interpretation is taken from a sermon preached by Wolcott Calkins, D.D., then minister of the Eliot Church in Newton, before the Massachusetts State Conference in Holyoke on June 17, 1890.

is here defined by two words which are technical and startlingly ceremonial.

The first of these is the noun "minister." It is a rare word, defining the highest and most sacred task of the appointed ministers of Jesus Christ. Its literal meaning is "a worker for the people." The word had a long and sacred history, dating from celebrations of victory in ancient Greece and from it our English word "liturgy" is directly derived. The Christian liturgist, according to the Apostle, is one who is offering in his preaching thanksgiving to God for victory over sin and death, while the people offer the wealth of their prayers and devotion. Thus preaching itself is the Church's liturgy of worship. The other is a different word, the participle "ministering." The Greek word is not found elsewhere in the New Testament. The first part of the compound means "a priest" and the second part means "to work." Thus preaching is to do priestly work. Here is no distinction so often made between priest and prophet. The prophet is the priest at work; the sermon is a sacrament. Preaching is nothing less than preparing the only sacrifice which can ever be offered to God, the broken and the contrite heart, for himself, for his people, for the world. Hence preaching the gospel is worship. At its best, it is the highest and most sacerdotal form of worship, the divinest liturgy of the Christian Church, in which preacher and people are united in one ascending sacrifice of contrition and oblation of thanksgiving.

This definition of preaching as worship reveals the innermost nature of the sermon. It is a communication of the grace of God through the lips of the preacher. Thus true preaching always has its mystic character. The grace of God is communicated to the believer in other ways: through his own direct approach to God in prayer and devotion; through the intangible influence of the sanctuary when he finds himself in the midst of its hoarded beauty in the company of his fellowmen; when he receives the sacrament at the moment of holy communion. But the grace of God is also transmitted directly to human lives when this is incarnate in the preacher and is uttered by him into human ears. There is possible this transference of truth and reality from one man's mind and heart, in the grip of an actually felt experience of that grace, to other men's minds and hearts. Only this actual transmission of grace can be defined as true preaching. All real preaching has this sacramental nature. Faith, to use again Dean Inge's well-known phrase, is not taught, rather it is caught. One of the most beautiful and mystical moments in spiritual experience is the response of the human heart to the felt grace that is communicated to it by the preacher out of the realities of his own experience of it.

If this be the sermon, then what must be the preacher? Evidently he must be one who feels that the grace of God has been given him that he may declare it to the people. This interior grace must be his own possession before he can seek to transmit it. This is the innermost qualification of the preacher. Without it all else is as sounding brass and a tinkling cymbal. This "grace" will be clothed in a form in which all other kinds of knowledge enter. It will have in and about it material drawn from many sources; it will be directed to various forms of human experience. But the thing itself, the mystical reality of the life and love of God in Jesus Christ, that must always remain warm and glowing at the very center of the preacher's being, and in and through himself offered to the people. It is for this that the people wait. And it does not take them long to tell whether or not the preacher himself knows what he is talking about. Laymen sometimes distrust the clergy because they feel that ministers seem to attain to "great experiences" too easily and use great words for what is not inwardly and actually and deeply experienced. But let them be convinced that with real humility and however feebly and haltingly the preacher is seeking to pass on to them a reality which has truly entered into and mastered his own nature, of the truth and eternal significance of which he is passionately persuaded, and they will not only listen but gratefully receive that grace and offer the sacrifice of thanksgiving that is well-pleasing to God.

The days in which we live offer unparalleled opportunities to the Christian preacher. Preaching always comes to the front, is given its finest chance for influence, is allowed to climb to the summits, when the external conditions of life are disappointing, bewildering, and depressing. Such is the hour for which the gospel was made, and in which the proclamation of the gospel should be a joy and a spiritual triumph. Ministers of Christ's religion in these days should hear a trumpet-call that summons them to their task, and the tone of their utterance should give out no uncertain sound. Men are suffering today from mental and moral depression. A mood of pessimism and of cynicism has replaced that of hope and of faith. Here, then, is a popular mood in which preaching ought to shine like a bright and burning light and in which the proclamation of the everlasting gospel should rise to its heights. The true preacher today will not linger on surface themes, nor will he make helpful deductions from current events. Rather he will draw his inspirations from the deepest sources and proclaim a faith that is rooted in the moral nature of God himself.

The sermon will have a certain fullness and richness. It will be full of human interest and not a series of abstractions. It will betray a certain breadth of culture, a knowledge not only of literature but of life. Its illustrations will be drawn from personal experience, observation, and reading. The preacher gives the impression that he has limitless material at his disposal. He does not indulge in much quotation. On this point Bishop Quayle has wisely written: "If the preacher holds books in solution in his brain so that he is not himself a book in a different binding, but that books enter into his vitalities and on any day can burgeon in him with a hidden gladness, then is a preacher safe with his books; but if they tyrannize over him like some children do over their fathers, then will the book be a millstone hanged about his neck. And what may happen to a man with such neckgear is common knowledge." [2]

[2] Bishop William A. Quayle, *The Pastor-Preacher*, p. 42. Abingdon-Cokesbury Press, publishers.

The sermon is always interesting. It is interesting in the manner in which it is uttered, in the material which goes into it, above all because it impinges directly upon some human interest, some human problem, some human need. It is directed to serve human beings. A true sermon always has humanity within it and divinity behind it.

Good sermons usually have a long history. They mature slowly. They are not made between Sundays. A week is too short a time for an idea to germinate, grow, blossom into full bloom. Hence the preacher is constantly jotting down ideas for sermons as these come to him in his study of the Bible, his reading, his observation. These are labeled and put away for future use. The material is constantly added to from time to time until it becomes quite bulky. The preacher's mind is like a boy's pocket, "stuffed with miscellaneous treasures of which his elders are not worthy: string, marbles, peg-tops, strange shells, bits of colored pebble, a few old coins of no seeming value, treasures strictly personal to himself, a chaos of which with glee, he, the boy, knows no one can make a cosmos but himself." Just so the preacher out of odds and ends garnered over a considerable period of time at length fashions his sermons, which may have been months or even years in maturing. Perhaps he knows few hours of deeper delight than when he pours all these treasures out on his desk and lovingly puts them together into the sermon which then he yearns to preach. He runs up the pulpit stairs with it. The preacher will have scores of sermons thus slowly maturing. His question is not what to preach, but only what to preach next. It is said of Henry Ward

Beecher that he would stroll out towards the end of the week into his homiletical orchard and survey the fruit, picking at last what seemed all ripe and ready and using it, leaving the rest until it should fully ripen also.

The preacher will be a continuous and profound student of the Bible. To the neglect of the Bible may be traced many of the shortcomings of the pulpit. Too much modern preaching has lost touch with the Bible. It does not talk in Bible language, it does not deal with Bible themes, it does not proclaim the Bible message. So much that goes by the name of preaching is not really preaching at all. It is good talking; it offers good advice; it advances sound morals; it comments helpfully on personal and social problems. But it lacks the authentic note of Christian preaching, which is the reproduction of the Bible message with its dominant themes of justice and mercy, of sin and salvation, of human need and divine redemption. Many preachers, because they think they must be modern, feel they must not be too closely bound to the Bible, which is ancient. As a matter of fact, the Bible is both ancient and modern. Its message is essentially timeless. What went on in the family of Jacob is going on in many a modern home. The Psalms are today the confessional of the world. The messages of the prophets, major and minor, when disentangled from temporary historical and political details, have almost startling relevancy to the problems of our day. Everything that seems archaic in the letters of Paul is like a fly-speck on a page which teaches the only ethic that can meet the issues of our modern world.

No other era in Christian history so needed Bible

preaching as the day in which we live. We need to listen once more to the voices of the prophets, heralds, and apostles who are announcing not the theory of a day, but the eternal truth which came to them as a fresh revelation of the will of God. Above all, we need to hear the voice of Jesus. The preacher who allows his academic uncertainties concerning the authenticated words of Jesus to prevent him from proclaiming the essential gospel as it is in Christ is unworthy of his calling.

Bible preaching never runs dry or grows thin. The Bible is indeed a well of living water into which the preacher may dip his bucket at will and find it full to overflowing. The topical preacher, the one who is always hunting for a theme, may find himself cudgeling his brains about next Sunday's sermon. But never the Bible preacher. Out of his knowledge of it, out of his deepening familiarity with it, out of constant fresh reading and study of it, there comes increasing wealth of material, all of it fitted to what the preacher knows to be the immediate and pressing needs of those to whom he is commissioned and privileged to preach. There are never enough Sundays in the year for Bible truths that clamor for utterance.

Expository preaching is rich with possibilities both for the preacher and for the congregation which delights in it. By this is not meant a long series of sermons from one Bible book, but occasional sermons expounding some portion of Scripture. Sometimes the preacher will take an entire book for his subject: Esther, Ruth, Ecclesiastes, one of the minor prophets, Philemon or Titus or the book of Revelation. It is a fine homiletical exercise for the preacher, and it makes the Bible book live once more for his hearers. Such sermons are likely to be among those longest and most gratefully remembered. Sometimes he will take one of the Old Testament stories, so rich in human interest, or incidents out of the Gospels which are filled with spiritual truth; or again he will choose a whole chapter like Ezekiel 37 or Acts 10, and set these down in the light of their eternal meanings.

All such preaching is interesting. It is also fructifying. It touches always on the permanent issues of life. And it gives the Bible back to the people. There are whole areas of the Bible with which church-going, Bible-reading Christians are not familiar and into which they seldom venture. Right here lies the opportunity of the Bible preacher. He will clear away the debris, reveal the truth that is eternal within these neglected portions of Scripture, and open up before his grateful hearers new and spacious pastures of delight of whose existence they were not aware. When they go home they will take up their Bibles and read them with new understanding. A college student was found reading his Bible after attending church one Sunday when the preacher had expounded the book of Obadiah. Feeling that some explanation was needed, he said he wanted to see how the preacher got all that out of it. Probably he was not the only member of the congregation who took up his Bible that day, for to many it is still a chained book as it was before the Reformation.

Preaching will not be an unrelated series of sermons throughout the year. It will be planned carefully for its inclusive educational effect. A layman once said to his minister: "I perceive architecture in your preaching." At the end of the parish year the preacher should feel that he has taken his congregation over the whole content of Christian truth, not neglecting any essential part of it. To this end the cycle of the Christian year should be followed with its successive seasons of Advent, Christmas, Epiphany, the pre-Lenten and Lenten period, Easter and the following Easter weeks, Ascension, Whitsunday, and the Trinity festival which celebrates the completion of the Christian truth.

The preacher will sit down early in the fall and map out his sermons before Advent. These will deal with subjects which bear directly upon the duties and privileges of the individual in the cultivation of his own spiritual life and his responsibilities as churchman and citizen. The dates will all be carefully filled in down to Advent. Then will follow sermons in preparation for Christmas and running down to the New Year. Before Lent, the theme will be the universalism of the Christian message, the missionary ideal, the inclusiveness of the Christian evangel which touches every aspect of human experience. "Gospel sermons" will always be preached in Lent, and the Sundays into June will all be shaped according to the message of the seasons that follow.

Thus the preaching will be carefully planned long in advance. The preacher will always know weeks beforehand what he will do. This schedule is always subject to alteration and revision, for the spirit bloweth where it listeth and inspiration is subject to no rule or regulation. But at least there will be continuity and constructiveness in such preaching and the preacher is always spared any uncertainty and anxiety concerning his work.

Incidentally it may be remarked that the all but universal habit of announcing the topics of sermons in advance has certain serious drawbacks and even positive objections. For one thing it commits the preacher to a subject and thus leaves no latitude for the tides of the spirit. And again it encourages one of the most dismal practices in modern Protestantism — the going of people from this church to that to hear what this, that, or the other preacher will have to say on a theme which attracts their attention. The sermon is an integral part of the worship of the Church, but it is not an end in itself.

Preaching is the most difficult of all tasks. The delivery of a sermon makes enormous demands on physical, nervous, mental, and spiritual energy. "Some doctors say that it is equivalent to two days' manual labor. Preaching is as critical as surgery and as sacramental as Calvary. When the sermon is over the minister feels that virtue has gone out of him, even as did his Lord." [3] Ruskin once said that the preacher has no more than thirty minutes in which to raise the dead. Therefore the preacher approaches his task with all the strength that is his. He prepares himself with all possible care and diligence. He does not leave the making of his sermon until Saturday afternoon. If he does, as Phillips Brooks once remarked, his congregation will likely wonder why it took him so long to prepare it. Of Thomas Shepard, Cotton Mather writes thus in his *Mag-*

[3] "As the Minister Sees It" by Howard J. Chidley in the *Seminar Quarterly*, August 1940.

nalia: "He was a very studious person and a very lively preacher; and one who therefore took great pains in his preparation for his public labors — with respect whereunto he once used these words: 'God will curse that man's labors that lumbers up and down in the world all the week and then upon Saturday in the afternoon goes into his study, whereas God knows that time were little enough to pray and weep in, and get his heart into a fit frame for the duties of the approaching Sabbath.' "

No greater opportunity can be given to any man than to be able to speak once a week to a company of people, large or small, on the deepest issues of life. To no other man in the community is such a privilege given. John Robinson, in his last sermon preached at Leyden before the departure of the Pilgrims, used these words: "Every assembly is a time big with destiny. Every Sunday men and women go forth from their tryst with God to face nameless responsibilities. Before the week is out, some may have launched their Mayflower and embraced a God-given adventure." So every true preacher faces his congregation. No assembling of ourselves together ought ever to be called ordinary. There was no single element present in that Leyden meeting house that may not be present at any hour of worship. The occasion is truly extraordinary in the spiritual possibilities which it presents. To speak out of one's own experience what may brace men to meet life victoriously — such is the romance of preaching.

CHAPTER 13

And from House to House

W HEN in his immortal valedictory to the elders of the Church at Ephesus Paul said: "I taught you publicly," he did not come to a full stop. The sentence does not end with a period. He went right on to say "and from house to house." His preaching, in a word, was not confined to the pulpit. He took his message from house to house. He did not feel that his work was done when he had preached a sermon to a congregation. He must take his spiritual treasure into the intimacies of the home and apply it to the needs of men and women as these were disclosed to him as he met them by themselves. Yet this too was preaching, but by the conversational method. The apostle appears to say distinctly that if he had preached publicly only, there would have been something lacking. And so he adds: "and from house to house."

Thus closely are the preaching and the pastoral offices of the minister linked together. Often they are regarded as things apart. The minister has his sermons to prepare and to deliver. That is one part of his task. But then he has his parish calling to attend to. And the two do not seem to be closely related to each other. He begrudges the time he must spend in parish visitation. He would like to spend it in reading and in sermon preparation. He would prefer a parish which did not expect "too much calling" of its minister. This distinction, however, between the offices of preacher and pastor is short-sighted and unscriptural. Real preaching is not over when the sermon has been preached publicly. And only the preacher who has learned as he goes from house to house what are the deepest needs of his people, will be able to preach effectively in public.

The preaching is never over when the Sunday sermon is at an end. People sit and listen. But they have no opportunity to interrupt, to question, to voice doubt or dissent. They go their several ways, carrying their unvoiced impressions with them. But now let the minister follow them from house to house. Then the sermon can be continued if reference is made to it or a new sermon can be preached that will come nearer to the heart. A minister preached once at the Thanksgiving season from Paul's extraordinary words: "Giving thanks for all things." Then he went to a certain house wherein was a woman who was facing stark tragedy in her life with which, although she did not know it, he was perfectly familiar. "After all," she said, "there are some things for which one could never give thanks." "I suppose," he replied, "you mean the wrong-doing of one whom one loved." She shot him a swift glance. "You know, then," she said. And another sermon was preached in that house, but not publicly.

Again, parish visitation is the one sure means of gathering invaluable homiletical material. To preach effectively, a minister must possess various forms of knowledge. He must have his own first-hand knowledge of God. He must know his Bible from cover to cover. He must be acquainted with the ruling ideas of the world in which he lives. But also he must know men where they are and have personal acquaintance with the problems and difficulties that are vexing their souls. Much preaching is wholly ineffective because it does not grapple with any live human problem.[1] It discusses themes which are remote from actual human experience. It is immaculate and innocuous. A true sermon within a few sentences rivets the attention of the congregation because it is apparent that the preacher is to come to grips with a subject that his listeners have been wrestling with, a problem which they have not been able to solve. By what means shall he know what these problems are? By general observation, no doubt, and by reading of modern literature. But above all by meeting people intimately in their homes and listening to what they have to tell him of their hopes and fears. The greatest sermons that have ever been preached have had their source and inspiration in pastoral visitation. When Paul preached publicly, he was preaching what he had learned as he went from house to house.

Thus pastoral visitation is far from being a pastoral chore to be accomplished out of deference to a traditional demand which often seems to be unreasonable and time-consuming. It is not a routine affair, an effort to "cover the parish" within the parish year. Rather, rightly understood, it makes the deepest appeal to the imagination. It becomes a thing of unending and romantic interest. The minister looks forward to an afternoon of it with keenest spiritual expectation. He knows that he is going to learn something that he did not know before and something of the profoundest interest and meaning. He can tell within a short time after entering a home if he is going to find

[1] See "What Is the Matter with Preaching?" by Harry Emerson Fosdick, *Harper's Magazine*, July, 1928.

anything there. If not, the visit is friendly, brief, and uneventful and he moves on to the next house. Yet rarely will he return home without having come face to face with some problem that palpitates with human interest.

On entering a home, he will skilfully direct the conversation so that it will not be wasted on incidentals. He will ask, in a casual manner, questions that may uncover what lies on the heart of the one to whom he is talking. "All gone well since I was here last?" "You have had no hurdles to take lately?" Yet often there is no need of questioning. If one carefully and prayerfully prepares himself for this delicate mission, he will find that his feet are directed to the houses where he is most needed. "I felt sure that you would come to see me soon." "Do you know, I was looking for you for I needed you so much." Some calls will be over within a quarter of an hour. Others may last an indeterminate length of time. It all depends upon what one finds when he gets there.

To have, thus, the right of entrance into the home, into the life of the family, into the confidences of those for whom he cares, who know that he cares for them, this is unspeakable privilege to be used in all reverence and with deep regard for its inmost meanings.

In the old days, no pastoral call was supposed to be complete unless prayer was offered in the home. That custom will hardly be followed today. Except in case of special emergency, the minister will not use prayer in general parish visitation unless it is desired and asked for. Intuition must guide the minister in the occasional exceptions to this rule.

He will plan this visitation not in mechanical but in human ways. Perhaps the method least to be commended is that of printing on the church bulletin or otherwise announcing certain streets on which in the coming days his calls will be made. The assumed advantage is that he will be more likely in this way to find his friends at home. These, however, may have made other plans for those days. Yet, feeling that he will be affronted if he finds no one at home, they reluctantly alter their schedules, remain at home, and may even provide some light refreshment. About to start on his rounds, the minister is summoned by telephone to a distant hospital, and this emergency errand takes all afternoon. Meanwhile his impatient parishioners await the arrival of the minister who never comes.

Some ministers plan their parish visits on a yearly basis. They must "cover the parish" within the year. This, they calculate, will require the making of at least six visits on four afternoons of each week. So they block it all out and try hard to keep up to their schedule, allowance being made for absences and other duties. The trouble with this method is that the minister is likely to have his mind riveted on his schedule, rather than on what he finds as he enters the home. He must be out of it within the half-hour if the six visits are to be made. Hence he is not in a relaxed and receptive mood, with time a negligible element, intent only on seeing what is to be found there and ready to spend the entire afternoon on one visit if the occasion calls for it. Moreover, he is unable to avoid giving the impression of haste and this precludes at once the giving of confidences which are imparted only in an atmosphere of leisure. Real "preaching from house to house" can never be accomplished on a statistical basis.

Hence, one will proceed differently. Visits will be planned according to the evident need of them. Always there are the priority cases: the sick, the infirm, the bereaved. Then, there is the "stranger that is within the gates" to be welcomed, the bond at once to be established between him and the minister and the parish he represents. The minister, too, is constantly noting down names of persons who have detached themselves in some way from the rest, a visit with whom he feels will have special significance. Others will ask him to call, and these requests are immediately honored.

Thus the list of his calls stretches on from day to day and he is never at a loss to know where he will go. Perhaps no moment gives him more secret satisfaction than when, with a free afternoon before him, he takes out the list of his possible visits, looks it over prayerfully, and then decides where he will go that day, never knowing when he starts, however, whether he will make one visit or many, and not caring. For his idea is not to see how many visits he can make, but rather what he can accomplish as he goes "from house to house."

A woman once said half-reproachfully to her minister: "Do you know, you have not been inside my house for two years." "That is true," he replied, "and here is the reason. Every Sunday I see you and Mr. Marshall and Elizabeth and Edward sitting side by side in the church pew. Nothing has happened to disturb the peace of your home. I run across all four of you in the parish house every week. So I put in my time with the sick, the stranger, or the back-slider." "I see," she answered. But she was only half convinced. Within a short time her son fell dangerously ill. For two weeks the minister was inside that home every day. When the boy was declared out of danger, the mother followed the minister to the door. "Oh, do you remember what I said to you about not calling on us for two years, and will you forgive me? Now I understand." And most intelligent and experienced members of any parish do understand. Let a minister once acquire the reputation of being a faithful pastor, and no members of his flock will ever criticize him because he has not called on them. They will understand that all the while he has been busy with his "heavenly industries." The minister will not make it a point to call at every home each parish year. That may or may not be a possibility. Some homes may be "passed over" because "no plague hath come nigh that dwelling." But he will make it a point to see that no known need is neglected; that no opportunity of feeding the flock is lost.

A minister should early acquire an implacable pastoral conscience. That conscience once acquired will give him no rest, will never allow him to consider anything of greater importance or moment than attending to even the most inconspicuous case demanding pastoral attention. He will forego alluring opportunities for personal satisfaction of one kind or another, in order to minister to "one of the least of these." When Harvard University celebrated its Tercentenary, it conferred degrees upon outstanding men distinguished in science, literature, or the arts from all over the world. Among the men selected

for this unusual honor was Albert Schweitzer of Africa.
But he wrote that he was too busy caring for sick natives
on the Congo to come to Cambridge to receive the degree.
So he went undecorated by the University, but he surely
received a higher award than that.

The reading of the *Life of Alexander Whyte of Edin-
borough* by G. F. Barbour (N. Y. 1925, 7th ed.) is commended to all who aspire to be good pastors. There one
reads of indefatigable pastoral industry, exquisite and
penetrating sympathy, unending remembrance of individuals, unsparing expenditure of time and strength in
the care of his flock. A perfect example is held before
one of what consecrated pastoral enthusiasm may accomplish, the incalculable good it may do.

No one has opportunities for personal influence comparable to those of the parish minister. He plays the human
scale from top to bottom. There is no human emergency
where his influence may not be felt. He stands behind
the careless or wayward boy or girl and seeks to steady him
and guide him in right ways. He counsels and assists young
men and women in perplexity as to their future. He helps
many a family through days of financial difficulty, in times
of discouragement and failure. He is able to hold many a
home together when its peace and stability are threatened
through misunderstanding or wrong-doing. He lifts people
one after another, young and old, over obstacles in their
paths and helps them to bear burdens which only he knows
anything about.

Of such stuff are his days made as he goes "from house
to house." His opportunities for helpfulness are never-

ending and beyond what fall to the lot of any other. And all of this is done so quietly, so anonymously, that no one is aware of it, except those for whom it is done. And they never forget it. "I do not know" — the words were spoken by one who had been trying desperately to hold her home together — "I do not know what I should have done these last years if it had not been for my church!" And she was but one of many with this same feeling. Perhaps here is the reason why a social worker once remarked that the Church remains the one institution in the community to which the people as a whole still turn in love and loyalty. As time goes on, if a minister remains for years in the same parish, the relationship between him and his people grows richer and deeper. A young woman once summoned her minister on the death of her father. "Ellen," he said to her, "this is the sixth time that our lives have become linked": her confirmation, her marriage, the baptism of her child, and successive deaths in the home. What other relationships on earth can compare in meaning and beauty with the spiritual bonds between a true pastor and his people?

Consider a sample day in the life of a parish minister who knows his business in going "from house to house" and delights in it:

"I usually try to get started calling by two o'clock, but one thing you can be sure of is this: that the minister's life cannot be lived according to rule. As a matter of fact, the very first thing I did was to dictate some principles of baseball for the boys of the Church League baseball team to learn and follow. Before I had finished them, someone was waiting to see me. He wanted jobs beating rugs. I gave some names for him to follow up. Because I happen to be a member of the local school committee, I then rushed down to an exhibition of the handwork of the boys and girls in the special classes of the schools. While there, I saw and talked with a little Armenian girl who had lost her father a year ago and was left, at sixteen years of age, to take care of three or four younger children.

"Then in my car I picked up the wife of a sick parishioner and took her up to the hospital to see her husband. One of the head nurses stopped me in the corridor to talk about a problem in which we were both interested. Then off to see a faithful parishioner who had lost her son — practically her only support — to arrange a few details about the insurance. I called for some old magazines for the sick at another house; and from there went on to see a woman dying by inches with cancer of the throat; up another street to a family who had lately lost both a daughter and father. Going on some little distance, I stopped at a house where there was trouble with an older boy; and also the youngest, the baby, had not been baptized. Then to the Tuberculosis Hospital to see the matron there about an inmate, and also one of the nurses about confirmation.

"Back to pick up my 'fare' at the hospital, deposit her at home, and make a supper engagement at 5:30 at the General Electric Company, where the graduation exercises of the Americanization classes were to be held. Before the exercises were over, I had to leave to keep an appointment with a woman who had telephoned during the day. She told me a story which would make a splendid plot for a melodramatic movie. Really, one doesn't have to go to the movies to get thrills in the ministry. You get them all the time. Her story took half an hour or more and will need a lot of time to follow up.

"Upon arriving home again, a pile of mail that I had dictated in the morning awaited me to sign. Perhaps it would be interesting to run over the human contacts that came up in the letters dictated that day. Here are a few of them — not all, just a few: Answering a man who wanted to know where he could borrow $200; writing to a missionary who had gone out from the parish to work in the Panama Zone; assuring a young high school girl who is looking for work that her request had been remembered; writing a couple whom I had married — one a Roman Catholic, the other a Protestant — advising them about the baptism of their child; a letter to a sick man; another letter to a woman in great trouble.

"So it goes, practically every one of them dealing with some human problem — some concrete cases that had to be met. These, and a few other odds and ends attended to, brought it up to eleven o'clock and later. The clergy have no working union. They do not need it; they do not want it, because all their work is so varied, so compelling, so enticing, so attractive, so worth while, that one gets strength and satisfaction in the very doing of it." [2]

Take a day's work like that; remember that it is only one day in a year, and how can one estimate the incalculable good that is done, the unending satisfaction that is won by it? Pastoral work is an exciting, demanding, romantic adventure in life. It demands of a man that he be his best in every direction, in training of mind, in soundness of judgment, in fineness of character. Perhaps the best part of a minister's work is done, not when he preaches publicly, but "from house to house."

The life of a parish minister is unpredictable. He may draw up in advance the schedule of a day's work, but he never knows if he will follow it. A message may come at any time which will change the whole of it. Like the time-tables of our railways, it is "subject to correction and change without notice." This element of uncertainty, instead of being a hindrance in his work, actually adds to its

[2] This account, abbreviated from an article in the *Boston Sunday Globe*, was written by William Appleton Lawrence, now Bishop of Western Massachusetts, when he was pastor of St. Stephen's Church, Lynn.

zest and interest and fascination. Even the incessant ring-
ing of telephone or door bell is not an impertinence or an
annoyance, since each summons may be eloquent with
deepest meaning. He is in the mood of constant expectation and readiness for anything that may arrive at any
moment. And when it does, he swiftly reconstructs his
day. There is never any hesitation or hint of reluctance.
First things come first. No soul in need shall ever get
the impression that he has been inconvenienced in any
way in responding to its plea. The more of these messages
he receives, the happier he is.

"What a wonderful thing it is," he says to himself, "that
if people are in some real need, instinctively they think
of me and turn to me." The thing that would sadden him
more than anything else would be that his schedules were
undisturbed; that people should let him alone; that he
could go his own way, when all about him were troubled
and harassed lives in whose difficulties and needs he was
not permitted to share.

The deepest satisfaction in a minister's life is this constant, quiet, personal and spiritual ministration to all kinds
and conditions of men in every conceivable form of human
need. There lies an inexhaustible source of happiness. To
know it, one must idealize all of these separate tasks and see
in each one its eternal significance. A minister may lose the
most precious part of his possible experience unless he look
upon all of this as the best, the richest, the highest of all that
is given him to do. Some men serve parishes effectively by
good preaching and skilful administration but have neither
the will nor the ability to serve people individually. Such

men never know the deepest and most subtle joys of the ministry. To the man who has once found the satisfaction of pastoral experience, nothing can compensate for its lack. To solve one human problem, though it may require days of his time, is a far more significant performance, will yield him in the end far deeper satisfaction, and will make a far greater contribution to human welfare than to stand on any eminence to be seen and known of men.

It is nothing less than sheer tragedy if through lack of spiritual discernment, self-effacement, and love of men, a minister lose this, the crowning joy of his life. And also he loses the possibility of his deepest influence and the deepest gratitude of those to whom he ministers. To be loved, one must love much. The more one loves, the more he is loved. And the love that abides when all else has passed away is the love that bears, believes, and endures all things. A minister ought to have no higher ambition than to qualify as a faithful shepherd of his flock. The word "pastor" must be his highest title of honor. Indeed, there can be no higher; for only he has fulfilled the divine commission of his Lord: "Feed my lambs, feed my sheep," not only publicly, but "from house to house."

CHAPTER 14

Sick and Ye Visited Me

✠   ✠   ✠   ✠   ✠   ✠   ✠

I T is difficult for people in health and vigor who busily throng the streets and go energetically about their vocations to realize that in their midst is a large area of helpless invalidism; that thousands of people in homes and hospitals are lying sick, lonely, discouraged, and sometimes despairing in bed. Some of these are not there for long; others may have been there for months. Some are awaiting operations; some are slowly recovering from these; some are mentally infirm; some are suffering from fractures that will heal; others are awaiting the inevitable end. But all of them together live in a world unimaginably different from that in which those dwell who are in health and strength.

Here is an area of life of which few people in ordinary health have intimate knowledge. They have been ill themselves, but only for brief periods. They may have been patients in a hospital, but they did not stay there long. They have visited their sick friends, but these entrances into the world of invalidism have been infrequent and brief. Yet here is a world filled with people who need all the care and sympathy which can be mobilized in their behalf. A man who, out of vigorous health, had been for some months a member of this invalid community once said that it was like the entrance into a new world. "I never dreamed that such a world existed. When I leave here life will be a different thing for me from what it has been. I shall have a memory of things I had never understood. I shall know a sympathy which I had never felt."

It is the great privilege of the parish minister to enter freely, daily it may be, into this invalid world. He is given a right of entrance which is often denied to others. He is called upon to minister to these sick folk in the different conditions of mind and body in which they may find themselves. Only the physician has as intimate an acquaintance as he with this area of human experience. In this sphere of suffering he will do some of his most delicate and beautiful work. Here he will win some of his finest victories. Here, too, he will learn much of the hidden beauties of the human soul, of the heroism of which it is capable. He will make many spiritual discoveries in this land of invalidism. Entering it, he will feel like putting off his shoes, for the place whereon he stands is holy ground. To move about in such a realm as this is the highest form of romance.

Because this invalid world differentiates itself sharply from the normal life of the healthy and strong, so does visitation to those who inhabit it demand specialized knowledge, skill, care, and method. Hence those preparing for the ministry are now given instruction in this form of pastoral ministration, spend time in hospitals under competent supervision, learn by actual contact with the sick how best to care for them. Literature on the subject is available.[1] Parish ministers today are well prepared in advance for their delicate and important task of visiting the sick.

The minister visiting the sick will come to them not as

[1] The reader is referred to *The Art of Ministering to the Sick* by Richard C. Cabot and Russell L. Dicks. The Macmillan Company, 1936.

a psychologist or psychiatrist with tricks in his bag, nor even as the priest, except on rare occasions. Rather he will come as one human being to another. He will avoid all appearance of professionalism in attitude, voice, or manner. He brings not primarily the explicit and formulated consolations of religion, but religion itself as revealed in a personality that is imbued with insight, understanding, intuitive sympathy, and a certain spark and flame of life. The highest kind of service done for the sick is performed by this kind of personal ministration as distinguished from the particular offices of the clergyman. The exceptions to this rule concern very sick or dying persons or those who especially ask for and so receive the ministrations which only the minister is commissioned to give.

Some time ago, as a minister was leaving a patient, he ran into the doctor. They exchanged greetings and the minister went his way. When he next called on the patient the nurse said, "I have something to tell you. Do you remember when you last called that you met the doctor? Well, after you had gone he said to me, 'I always like to have that man call on my patients. For he always leaves them better than he found them.'" That is the test. A minister who has learned how to visit and care for the sick is able to communicate an inward reinforcement to the hidden spiritual forces of the invalid which makes for increased vitality and strength.

The first prerequisite of this is that the minister shall have within himself this possession of a strong, permeating, spiritual energy. He must be the bearer of a kind of life which is stronger than the alien forces that hold the body down. He must radiate out of his own fortified personality energies that communicate themselves to the sufferer. Unless this be true, anything he says or does will benefit little. But if this be true, whatever he says or does will raise the invalid to higher levels of hope and courage. Hence, he will enter the sick room as the conscious bearer of the strength that heals. And he will expect to expend that strength freely.

Patients are fully and instinctively aware of and sensitive to the personalities of their visitors. This is as true of doctors as of ministers. A woman who had been hopelessly ill for years was once visited years ago by a well-known practitioner in New York City. "He sat down by my bed," she afterwards said, "and looked at me in a way that was as far from a stare as anything could be. Then and for the first time I knew that I was going to get well." This undefinable but unmistakable power to transmit spiritual strength, to communicate spiritual hope, is the indispensable equipment of any minister truly qualified to minister to the sick.

But the approach to the invalid will always be quiet and gentle. There will be complete absence of suddenness, abruptness, or robustness that will be too severe a tax upon the resources of the sufferer. A patient once said that she positively dreaded the coming of a dear friend of hers because her friend's instant and exuberant vitality overwhelmed and crushed her. Health, it must always be remembered, is a temptation to inconsiderateness. One can exhaust the strength of one weaker than he by the very impact of his own unconcealed energy. Hence, when one enters a sick room, one will slacken speed. The step will be measured and restrained. One will give the impression of quietness. The voice will be gentle. One's whole powers will be held in leash, curbed and kept under strict control so as not to tax tender sensibilities and make too much demand upon the patient's weakened energies.

This gentleness is quite compatible with cheerfulness and brightness. Of a certain person Robert Louis Stevenson once said that when he came into a room it was as if another candle had been lit. Such must be the effect, gentle though it be, of the visit to the sick. It must brighten. A word or two: "You don't look very sick." "You had better make the most of this vacation of yours, for soon you will be getting back to hard earth again." "It must feel good to have nothing to do for awhile but lie still and be taken care of. There *is* a certain luxury in being sick, isn't there?" For a convalescent this will be all that will be needed. It adds a sense of brightness and of cheer. It quickens courage and increases a certain sense of comfort. It causes one to look at the silver linings in the clouds. The visit will be remembered with joy.

When a patient is more seriously ill, however, one will avoid pleasantries. One comes at once to grips with the situation. "You are having a hard time, are you not? Yet you know that everything is being done for you that skill and care can provide. I am going to help, too. Just remember that I shall be with you even when I am gone. There are all kinds of forces working in your behalf and on these you can rely. And you will cooperate with them, help and not hinder them, will you not? You will lay yourself down in peace and sleep, knowing that the Lord maketh you to dwell in safety, casting all your care upon him who careth for you."

The minister will not read from the Bible, but he will have at his command Bible verses that he can weave into his quiet and calming words, into his simple human speech. It is all quite different from formal devotions. Yet it ministers to the deepest needs and appeals to the deepest resources of his patient. The whole effort is directed to allaying tension, removing mental disturbance, bringing to pass a certain relaxation of both physical and nervous conditions hostile to that repose of mind and body that underlies the processes of recuperation and recovery.

As a rule, visits to the sick will be brief. Every precaution will be taken to prevent fatigue. Nurses sometimes dread the advent of a minister lest he stay so long as to tire the patient. Much better that the visit err, if at all, by being too short. Five minutes is often enough; sometimes ten; rarely over fifteen unless the patient is convalescent and needs diversion or has something on his mind that he wants to talk about. As a rule more good can be accomplished by a short visit than by a long one. If the patient is in bed, the minister will not sit down. The very fact that he sits down may start the suggestion that he is going to remain longer than the patient really wants or feels able to have him stay. Even if he is asked to be seated, he will take this as showing ordinary or desirable courtesy and he will decline. "Thank you, I do not mind standing. I am not going to stay very long. We can talk very well as it is." Thus the patient has no effort to make in addressing the visitor, who also has the advantage of observing the patient closely and detecting little signs that will aid him in adjusting himself to the patient's needs and knowing what the proper limit of his visit should be. Often the minister will bring a gift with him: a little book of cheerful verse, or a rose bud. "Sometimes," he may say, as he hands it to the patient, "one rose bud says more than a dozen."

If the visit is in a hospital ward with others lying near, the minister will never confine himself to the one whom he has come especially to see. Others may be looking on with hungry eyes, coveting for themselves what he has come to bring. So he passes from bed to bed with a word of cheer for each and he leaves behind him the benediction of his presence when he goes.

The minister will not discuss with the patient the nature of his illness nor its probable outcome. Here he will imitate the reticence of the nurse. If the patient inquires how he is getting on, and this he rarely does, the minister will reply: "Oh, now just don't ask me that. Ask the doctor. I am not an expert in those matters. But let us give the doctor a surprise by showing him how much you and I can do together. We can do a lot. Together we can come a long distance. What do you say?" He will seek to win the confidence and stimulate the faith of the sufferer. And such faith can move mountains. Also, the minister will never discuss the patient's condition with nurse or doctor while he is near the sick person or behind a closed door. If the patient feels that he is being discussed, that will rouse his suspicions and add to his anxiety. The visit over, the minister will leave at once and the patient will see and know that he does just that.

The preparation of a patient for an operation demands special skill. Fear and apprehension must be banished so far as the minister is able to do this by quiet talk and suasion. He will dwell on the extraordinary skill of the surgeon; on the way in which nature comes to the aid of the sufferer; on the necessity of resilience and ease of body and mind, of tranquility and hope. Often he will be able to induce sleep by this kind of quiet and reassuring ministration. The visit may well close with a simple prayer which speaks of God's enfolding care or the verse of a hymn such as "In heavenly love abiding no change my heart shall fear." Such forms of ministry have often quieted a patient when even sedatives have failed.

No rule or formula can determine whether a minister should pray with a patient or not. If he asks for it, the case is simple. If not, it is best not to inquire whether he wishes it. He may not really desire it, yet hesitates to say so lest it indicate that he has no felt religious need. Thus it is best for the minister to decide for himself. He may make a mistake either way. It is true that sometimes a prayer may induce the suggestion that the patient is very sick, sicker than he really is. It is also true, if the minister omits the prayer, that the patient who wants it all the while will wonder why. Intuition can be one's only guide. But if he prays, the minister will do well not to draw out a prayer book, or even to say "Let us pray." Rather, holding the patient's hand quietly and naturally, and without any introduction, he will either recite a prayer or offer one of his own, brief and simple for help and strength and life and healing. In maternity cases, prayer is plainly called for. Here is cause for thanksgiving of which the new mother is vividly conscious. Here is cause for consecration to the sacred task of the up-bringing of this new-made life. Here is cause for petition that mother and child may be defended from all danger and kept safe in God's peace. Such prayer is always welcomed and leaves its permanent impression.

Persistent cases of painful illnesses — sciatica, sclerosis, neuritis, rheumatism — require constant visitation, vigilance, and understanding. These invalids suffer in more ways than one. Their debilities become familiar to those in the household, whereas to themselves each day is fresh with poignant experience. No wonder, then, if they become mentally and morally depressed. A minister once went to see one of these sufferers whose days were never free from pain. As he entered the house, he met her sister, hatted, booted and spurred, ready for a pleasant afternoon engagement. "Oh," said the sister, "I am so glad that you have come. I know that you will say something to dear Sophie to comfort her." The minister was embarrassed because this was said *in her sister's hearing*. How could he find the right thing to say when he was instructed and expected to say it? He sat down. The invalid told him that her chief sorrow was that she was becoming irritable, rebellious. "I am glad to hear it," said the minister. "That shows that you have a healthy soul. If you could take this without rebelling against it, your soul would be as sick as your body. The more you rebel, the more you prove that you have a soul alive even if your body is infirm." She looked at him. "Do you mean that?" "Certainly, I do." "Well, then, that is the most comforting thing any one has ever said to me."

Such is the comfort to which this type of invalid is entitled. To bear pain daily and at the same time to repress the natural revolt against it should never be expected or demanded of man. Resignation and patience are indeed great Christian virtues. But they may deteriorate into a kind of passivity which dulls the fighting edge of the sword of the spirit, the finest weapon in the moral armory.

Mental cases demand special technique. Here some elementary knowledge at least of psychology and psychiatry is needed. At the root of obstinate melancholy, of nervous depression or mental confusion, there usually lies some obsession. One must discover the nature of it by repeated visitation, gradually acquiring the confidence of the patient and encouraging him to bring this out into full day and to expose it frankly. This may require some time. Next it will be pointed out that the patient must not blame himself for the fact of his obsession. The guilt complex must be removed. Then the faith must be established that the obsession is not irradicable. And finally, the patient must be persuaded to ignore it, to engage in some form of objective employment that will take the mind off one's self and provide outlet for congenial activities of both mind and body. Except in pathological cases, continued treatment of this kind will alleviate if it does not wholly cure the mental disease.

The minister will never hesitate to visit patients suffering from the most virulent forms of infectious or contagious diseases. Then he is most needed, for the sufferer is deprived of every other form of human companionship, with the exception of medical attendance. He will be admitted when all others are excluded. For him to hesitate to visit the sufferer because of the risk he plainly runs is to be disloyal to duty. He will take every precaution before and during and after his visits, following the direction of hospital attendants. But visit the patient he will, bringing with him the consolations needed for this extremity of human need. It is the rarest thing in the world for a minister thus courageously discharging his duty and performing the offices for which he was commissioned to be harmed in any way. Precisely as nurses protected by their own fortified personalities pass unscathed through contagious wards, so does he. And by so doing he not only has the consciousness of having lived up to the highest demands of his office, but he wins the undying gratitude of the patient as well as of the patient's family and friends.

In extreme cases, also, he will be prepared to celebrate the service of the Holy Communion. Sometimes this will be asked for by the patient. At other times, members of the family will request it or the minister will suggest it. For this purpose Roman Catholic and Episcopal clergymen are provided with what should be in the hands of every clergyman in dealing with the sick: an individual communion set. The sacrament in this use of it has well been called the "Viaticum," the provision for a long journey, and often it will give to a very sick or dying person the consolation and assurance which nothing else can bring. Now the minister is the priest.

As a matter of fact, he is always the priest, though he may not appear or act as one. For he bears as in an invisible chalice the very grace of God. He offers to the patient the very life of God. He is himself the living medium by whom and through whom the healing strength of God passes into the life of the sufferer. Hence the visitation of the sick becomes one of his highest and holiest tasks. The minister to whom this visitation is a routine duty to be performed because it is expected of him; who is himself depressed by what he sees; who is not conscious of any divine mission and does not expect to accomplish any divine results, knows nothing of the possibilities that lie before him. But the one who enters this realm of suffering deeply aware of his great privilege and opportunity, who is filled with the spirit of reverence at what he finds there, who equips himself with all the resources at his command and exercises his calling with all the care and skill that knowledge of both God and man can give him, can repeat the miracles of grace of him to whom no sufferer ever looked in vain.

CHAPTER 15

Ministers Unto Me in the Priests' Office

✠   ✠   ✠   ✠   ✠   ✠   ✠

S AUMUR is an old provincial town in France on the banks of the Loire. At the end of the sixteenth century it was one of the chief strongholds of Protestantism in France, and a Protestant church still exists there. To-day the town is chiefly important because of a large "Ecole de Cavalerie" established as long ago as 1768. At the entrance of the ancient Roman Catholic Church of S. Pierre, in the pre-war days, the traveler might have seen a placard urging French youth to enter the priesthood. It read in part: "There are just four great days in anyone's life: birth, confirmation, marriage, death. Would you not like to be one who would be needed on all four of those days?" Thus was set forth the unique glory and romance of the life of one who enters the ministry. He is commissioned, as priest, to bring the grace of God to human life in the critical hours of human experience.

The idea of the minister as priest has been obscured, for well-known reasons, in the thought and cultus of churches which have reacted against sacerdotalism, sacramentarianism, and catholicism in its ecclesiastical forms. But it is one that needs to be revived. For the minister is not only prophet commissioned to utter the oracles of God, he is also priest mediating between the soul of man and God. "The priest," said Carlyle, "is the uniter of the people with the unseen Holy; the ideal of him is that he be what we can call a voice from the unseen Heaven, interpreting the [mind and will] of God, unfolding the same to men."

All human experience proves the need of such a media-tion. The institution of the priesthood is as old as religion itself; that is, as old as humanity. Antedating the documents and records of religion, there was the priesthood. Today men may not have a religious literature or buildings or institutions, but always they have their priests. And always it is the priest who is needed to assure men of the near grace of God at the sacred hours of baptism, of initiation into the Christian community, of marriage, of death. Then the priest is indispensable. Only when ministers, besides being friend, visitor, preacher, are "ministers in the priests' office," do they realize the full significance of their mission to men.

Of course it is true that all true and righteous men may be mediators between God and their fellow men, may hear their confessions and help them to God. The "priest-hood of all believers" is not a pious fiction. In this sense the mere fact of ordination does not equip one to be a priest. Many people find their way to God and are assured of the forgiveness of sin through the example and minis-tration of saintly souls outside of the professional min-istry. Dwight L. Moody and Henry Drummond were never ordained. Yet they heard more confessions and pro-nounced absolution with greater assurance than any men, in or out of the ministry, of their generation. Such a min-istry is within the grasp of any devout soul that is clothed in the garment of holiness and equipped with insight, sympathy, and the authority which comes from deep and intimate faith in God.

When, however, we come to the sacraments, to the giv-

ing to the individual in visible form and symbol the grace
of God, there is an instinct in man which demands that
the person so offering grace shall be divinely and peculiarly
set aside for this office. It is true that this also has been
questioned and denied; that in some churches any devout
layman of unquestioned Christian faith and experience
is considered qualified to celebrate the sacraments. But it
is also true to say that this idea and practice does not do
justice to the normal and general religious consciousness.
This demands that there shall be a certain "apartness"
between layman and minister. Here is implied no theory
of apostolic origin or succession. Yet, however little ethically it may be justified, a line as thin as a hair but as
hard as a diamond must exist between the ordained minister and the godly layman. Only he who has been especially anointed and divinely appointed has the prerogative placed in his hands to perform this priestly function.
And here is something which may be better felt than rationalized. "Ordination includes a recognition of spiritual
gifts, and a commission to exercise these gifts in celebrating the sacraments in a given church. But it also
includes authority to act in the name and with the authority of the Church universal. And beyond that it confers
a sacramental character to the one so ordained. He is, not
in his personal character but only by reason of his office,
an effective symbol of the grace of God acting through the
Church." [1]

This idea, in turn, involves a certain conception of the

[1] See "Another Fifty Years?" by Angus Dun, in *Christendom*. Spring
Issue, 1943.

Church. The Church is not conceived as a company of Christian men and women who have voluntarily banded together for the purpose of Christian worship and instruction, in which the minister is simply one who has laid aside other employments in order that he may give himself wholly to the preaching and teaching of the Word and has no other position or authority than that derived from his own Christian experience and character. Rather the Church is regarded as the body of Christ, "the visible extension of the Incarnation," the supernatural home of the soul, the sphere of sacramental grace, the society which is Christ's visible witness and representative on earth in which he dwells, which his spirit guides and inspires. And the minister in such a Church is a man sealed to his vocation not of earth but of heaven and anointed divinely for the discharge of a sacred duty.

And this idea of the Church and the ministry in turn involves the conception of the sacraments as the medium through which divine grace is imparted to the human soul. This is not to say that the divine grace may not be received through channels other than the sacraments. Yet these are conceived as having an immediacy and as conveying a sense of the divine grace which is all their own. They enable the believer to penetrate beyond the sensible and lay hold of the divine reality; to be lifted out of the partial into the perfect, out of the temporary into the eternal, out of self into God. For the visible symbol has its supreme place in man's religious life.

Therefore from the very beginnings of Christian history the sacraments have had their central place in the worship of the Church. The actual and possible union of the life of God and man has from the first been visualized in things that could be felt and touched. And these have quickened the sense of the reality of which they are but the signs. Thus to minimize their meaning and influence in the Christian cultus is to deprive our human nature of one of its deepest necessities. To relegate the sacraments to a secondary and subordinate position in worship; to overlook the deep appeal to imagination, to the inward sense which appropriates directly the grace and truth of the life of God in Christ without rationalizing it, is to misunderstand the deepest needs of the human soul. We need to exalt the sacraments to their primary place in Christian worship, as visible signs and symbols of the divine grace, as a means of conveying it to the human heart. This is of the very essence of real religion.

The minister celebrating the sacraments will have an adequate conception of their meaning.[2] The essence of this is that *something has happened:* grace has actually been conveyed that the believer could not receive by any act of his own. By the exercise of his faith the divine reality is transmitted into his life. The Protestant tradition, in its revolt against what was felt to be a superstitious and unscriptural conception of the sacraments, lost the sense of objective reality and reduced their meaning to a purely subjective influence which some might feel and others not.

Yet while retaining intact fundamental Protestant prin-

[2] A full exposition of this idea by the author may be found in *The Seminar Quarterly,* February 1942.

ciples of the faith of the believer rather than the infallibility of the Church and priesthood as the guarantee of grace, the sacraments may and should be understood as possessing in themselves a divine reality external to the believer himself, but becoming his when in faith he receives them in a fashion which otherwise could not be his. In a word, it is necessary to believe that *something has happened* if the sacraments are to be given their proper dignity and meaning in Christian worship. When the sacraments are so conceived, their celebration by the minister is for him also a deeply mystical experience.

The baptism of infants was not the earliest practice of the Church, but came into general usage about the third century in the Christian era. As Protestants, we do not accept the Catholic doctrine, Roman or Anglican, that the child becomes miraculously regenerate in baptism, which is therefore necessary to salvation. But, if that idea is taken out of infant baptism, what is left? Very little, according to much opinion. It is a picturesque and beautiful rite. Every one is interested. It is indeed an act of consecration or dedication — a word often used as a substitute for the word baptism. But the sacrament is without actual significance. There is no realization that any real transaction has taken place. There is no objective reality in the sacrament.

Yet, as truly interpreted according to strict Protestant principles, something tremendous has happened. There has been celebrated the mysterious fact of the union of the life of man and the life of God, the fact of the divine paternity. Baptism does not create it, but affirms it. "This child belongs to the family of God and you do now recognize its birthright." That is a tremendous fact and baptism is the symbol of it. Thus a new dignity is lent to human life at its weakest and frailest hour. It is given a divine, a romantic valuation. The value of baptism in relation to this sublime truth is the value of all symbols. The immaterial truth is embodied in material form that we may see it and feel it. Again, in baptism water is used, the symbol of lustration, of washing. Thus there is symbolized the tremendous fact that there is a washing wherewith the soul may be cleansed no matter what defilement it may contract "in the midst of this miserable and naughty world." When a little child has water placed on its head, there is symbolized the romantic truth that no matter what may befall him in later life, given only faith, his soul shall be presented at the last pure and immaculate to God. If to this be added that parents, properly instructed, take solemn vows that the child shall be brought up "in the nurture and admonition of the Lord," the significance of the sacrament of baptism is evident.

Ministers will not refuse to baptize a child neither of whose parents are church members if they will make this vow and pledge themselves to keep it. And if they do, the likelihood is that they too eventually will be led into fellowship with the Church. The practice of assembling as many infants as possible for baptism on Children's Day, at Easter, or some other one Sunday in the year is to be discouraged. For one thing, the occasion thus becomes something of a spectacle which detracts from the deeper meanings of the event. Again this prevents a more frequent repetition of the rite, which has a powerful educational effect on the congregation. If parents prefer an anniversary day, their wishes will be followed. Otherwise, the children will be brought separately on any Sunday convenient to them. Baptisms will always be inscribed in the parish and pastoral records, and parents will always be given a baptismal certificate.

The rite of confirmation, the act whereby an individual unites with the Church, is commonly celebrated in connection with the Holy Communion. Only in Roman Catholic and Episcopal churches is it an office by itself. For this act of dedication the individual will be carefully prepared and its full significance will be explained. He is not merely becoming a member of the local church; he is not only joining a given denomination, thus becoming a Methodist, a Congregationalist, or a Presbyterian; rather he is being taken up into "the blessed company of all faithful people," becoming a very member incorporate in the mystical body of Christ, which is the Church. He joins the innumerable company of those who in all times and in all places have confessed the name of Christ and thus form the Holy Catholic Church which is the communion of saints. To be taken up into such a universal society of the friends of Jesus is the greatest dignity which can come to a human life. Henceforth he is a member not of one church, but of all churches, which together form the Church Universal. This must be so envisaged by the candidate that the day on which it takes place becomes to him the greatest day of his life. In that Church, visible and invisible, he will abide in time and in eternity.

No one can be urged to take such a step. It must come of his own glad, free choice and acceptance as a precious privilege which he cannot forego. His surrender to Jesus Christ must be complete, so that henceforth Christ in him becomes the hope and the promise of his glorification. Neither the intellectual acceptance of formal statements of faith nor religious emotionalism of any particular type will be required. But there will be this searching demand for uncompromising loyalty to Christ. This from the beginning has been the one condition of Christian discipleship, of admission into the fellowship of Christ's Church. "Let him deny himself, take up his cross, and follow me."

Thus the service when this act of consecration, of initiation into the spiritual society which is the Church takes place will be invested with all possible solemnity, will be accompanied by beauty of circumstance, and will be conducted by the minister with profoundest personal feeling. Indeed, when he considers the romantic possibilities bound up in those lives in whom Christ abides, no service which he is called upon to perform evokes deeper emotion.

The Lord's Supper, according to common Christian usage, is the central rite of the Church. From the first it was incorporated in the worship of the Church as having been instituted and enjoined by Christ himself. "This do in remembrance of me." But while Christians agree in their observance of this sacrament, they differ widely in their interpretation of its meaning. According to the Catholic view, Roman and Anglican, the Church is an outward and visible entity, authenticated in history by its apostolic priesthood, apart from which no sacrament can have ultimate validity or convey actual grace. The one true and only Church enshrines within it the sacrament, the gift of grace which can be transmitted and bestowed only through its own accredited and appointed priesthood. Thus the believer may receive it in full assurance that he is receiving the fact of salvation. The multitudes kneeling in adoration at the celebration of the Mass feel within their souls that something tremendous is happening: their soul's deliverance from sin and death.

The Protestant Church has never possessed a generally accepted doctrine of the meaning of the Lord's Supper. As a result, many Protestant believers have a very vague and incomplete idea of the meaning and significance of this central rite of the Church. It was instituted by our Lord. It should be observed by all Christians. One should approach the Lord's table with reverence. Yet they are not deeply aware of its effect upon themselves or of its necessity as conveying or giving them anything which they could not otherwise possess. The average Protestant congregation needs thorough re-education into the profound significance, meaning and necessity, clear and understandable, of this sacrament. This process of education will proceed from what is at once evident to what is not clearly apprehended. It is, then, in the first place a simple, commemorative rite, a memorial of the suffering and death of Christ, a devout calling before the mind of how Christ did suffer and die *for us*. The mind is turned backward.

The value of the sacrament lies in its vivid presentation of the willing sacrifice of Love for all of us, and in the upleap of the answering love of the Christian heart to that supreme sacrifice.

Again, there is the conception of the indwelling life of Christ as a spiritual fact and principle, the passing over from the person of Christ into the person of the believer of the vitalizing power of his spirit. We are reminded vividly by the use of these holy symbols that just as food and drink are necessary to sustain the body, so the inward spirit of Christ, which we symbolically appropriate in the act of eating the bread and drinking the wine, is necessary for the nourishment of the soul. Thus the Christian is taught that the Christian life cannot be lived by the mere moral effort to follow after Christ, to keep his precepts and daily to imitate his example. It can be lived only from Christ as the inward center of our inspiration. Only dependence upon Christ and the nourishment of the soul by Christ avails to Christian living. This idea of the sacrament is also an early one. It is clear and intelligible, and it is generally accepted and agreed to by all Protestant Christians.

But there is a third interpretation, well within Protestant principles, to which most Protestants have not yet arrived, which is necessary for a re-establishment of the sacrament to its rightful place and meaning. If its full significance is to be realized, the transition must be made from its subjective influence upon the heart of the believer to its objective reality. Only in this way can the Protestant as well as the Catholic believer feel that in the celebration of the sacrament something really happens. We need, in a word, the recovery of the idea of the presence of Christ in the sacrament. The rejection of the idea of a physical miracle whereby the bread and wine become the very Body and Blood of Christ, does not necessarily involve the rejection of the spiritual concept that Christ himself is present in the sacrament. "The bread remains indeed bread, and the wine remains wine. But in their use and in their effects the bread is as if it were the body, and the wine as if it were the blood of Christ."

Hence, not because mediated by an infallible Church or priesthood, but because of the faith of the believer, he may know that in receiving the sacrament, he is laying hold on Christ himself. One can lay hold on Christ as truly by partaking of the bread and wine as if Christ himself were there in his bodily presence. Thus the sacrament does more for the believer than to point to an historical event in the past or to help him to realize the fact of the inward renewing spirit of Christ. It presents to him Christ himself, that is, salvation. And the determining fact which makes possible this miracle of Christ present is nothing exterior to the believing heart, but rather the felt faith of that heart. This works the miracle of the real presence of Christ in the sacrament.

This idea, still indistinct if not foreign to the average Protestant consciousness, must be recovered if the sacrament is to be raised to its full dignity and given its full significance. When the minister feels that his is the divine prerogative of placing in men's hands and to their lips Christ himself who is our salvation, he rises to the full realism of his commission as "a minister of God in the priests' office."

The Holy Communion will be celebrated with all possible dignity and reverence. It will never be an addendum to the service which precedes it. Rather it will be the very center and heart of that service. Where the Order is not prescribed, it will be carefully studied, with all the aids which are now available for that purpose, and every detail will be planned to give the service its impressive meaning. The minister himself must be filled with the sense of its significance. The communion service in the so-called non-liturgical churches will be held at least once in the month. On alternate months an early celebration, without address, may well find its place in the cultus of the church, as well as occasional celebrations on Holy Thursday, at Easter, and on Christmas day. Thus the congregation will be educated in the meaning and use of the sacraments as a central fact in the ministry of the Church to their souls. The ordering of the Lord's Table will be cared for by a special group carefully trained for this sacred office.

The marriage service is one which no true minister approaches without realization of its profound meaning. Here is to be inaugurated a new family, the very foundation of our whole social order. Here is to be consummated the union of two human lives, thenceforward to belong exclusively each to the other. Here is to be witnessed the fusion of two divergent personalities into one comprehending unity by the alchemy of a mutual love.

Here by divine grace is to be performed the miracle of
Cana of Galilee, the transmuting of the material, rational,
and judicious considerations which lead two people to
agree to throw in their lot together, into the pure and high
romance of a truly spiritual relationship. Therein lies the
difference between a civil and a church marriage. Therein
also lies the explanation of the vast difference between the
frequent dissolution of civil marriages and the proud
record of the permanent and happy homes created by the
Church.

Thus, the minister approaches the marriage service in
a wholly different mood from the justice of the peace. The
latter is concerned only that legal requirements are fulfilled. It is a casual appointment. He goes through the
forms and wishes the couple well. His duty is over. Far
different is the attitude of the Christian minister. Here
is a sacrament to be performed, not only with the ritual,
but with the benediction of the Church. Here grace is to
be bestowed, a divine, spiritual power by which those
virtues shall be practiced and upon which the blessings of
a true marriage shall be won. Kneeling before the altar,
man and woman pledge to each other a love which is only
possible because of the Love which embraces them both.
They have as they leave the Church the gift in their hearts
which shall enable them in the vicissitudes of life to experience an inward principle of spiritual affection which
shall bind them closer and closer together. Here is a union
of lives founded not on prudential reasons, but on the
very grace of God.

All of this will be set forth to those about to be married

in a quiet pre-nuptial talk by the minister. He does not content himself with a "rehearsal." He must have those who are to enter into this sacred and enduring relationship understand its spiritual meaning. They must see and feel that a true marriage makes its inevitable moral demands. It requires that each shall exercise the high virtues of generosity, unselfishness, consideration, courtesy, thoughtfulness, the willing surrender of one's own desires and preferences, "in honor preferring one another." One cannot have a true home and at the same time have his own selfish way. Selfishness is the nemesis of marriage. The very concept of marriage involves the capacity to live unselfishly. Yet what one gives up is as nothing to what one receives. As each studies to make the other happy, he receives in return unimaginable happiness. All of this is possible, yet possible only as the grace of God abides in the heart. Hence the dedication of their lives to God should precede the dedication of their lives to each other. This is the essence of a true Church marriage, and the blessing of the Church contains the gift of grace whereby they shall be so able to live together that the unearthly joy of a true marriage may be theirs. The marriage service will be read over and carefully explained. A prayer will conclude the interview. Such a prelude to the marriage service is always welcomed and it makes its profound impression.

The question whom the minister shall marry must be decided by his own conscience within the laws of the State and of the Church to which he belongs. He will well hesitate, and even decline, to marry total strangers, especially if they are young and can offer no reasonable explanation why they were not married in their own homes or communities. He will seek to safeguard the sanctity of marriage by every means in his power. He will never marry anyone without an interview and without full knowledge of all the facts. If he marries any persons whose parents do not approve the marriage, he will know just reasons for so doing. Sudden marriages will be discouraged except in emergencies. Every marriage will be entered in the parish register and the minister's own records.

The matter of mixed marriages will be handled by the minister with unusual care. The marriage of a Jew and a Christian presents few difficulties if neither objects to the form of service used. The bride will have the choice, and will be married by rabbi or minister as the case may be. In the case of a Roman Catholic and Protestant, the bride again must make the decision. If she is a Roman Catholic the marriage will be by the priest, and to this the Protestant groom will give his consent. If she is a Protestant, it is possible that the Roman Catholic groom will consent to marriage by a Protestant minister, although the laws of his church do not permit it. Otherwise the bride, though a Protestant, will consent to be married by the priest. This her minister will not discourage. She will have been married within the Church, although it be not her church, to which she may and should continue to be loyal.

The service itself will be read with great deliberation and profound feeling. "A minister should be trained in ceremonial. The great occasions of life call for recognition and formal expression. To celebrate them inadequately is felt to be a grievous error. The instinct which demands a church wedding is more than a desire for the social decencies. The secular prose of things falls short of our major joys and sorrows on festivals and anniversary days. Man cries out for poetry, and ceremonial is the answer to this cry."

The funeral service is the hardest task the minister has to perform, and he will never get used to it. Each funeral will be to him a totally new and fresh experience, precisely as if he had never conducted one before. The news that death has entered a home causes him at once to feel the sanctity of the event. He will enter upon his duties with profound insight and sympathy and equip himself with all the spiritual resources at his command. A man once remarked that the funeral service for his mother was, for the minister who conducted it, "just another funeral." That ought never to be true. Death is indeed in one sense a commonplace. The death columns appear in the papers fresh with new names every day. But each one of those names represents a heartbreaking experience for someone, and the hour when the service is held is a sacramental one filled with most poignant spiritual experience and to be approached by the minister with the utmost reverence.

Always he will call on the family in advance and adjust the service to their desires. Scrupulously he will attend to every detail, to avoid any possible infelicity. He will take infinite pains. He will prepare himself carefully, having regard to every circumstance coming within his knowledge of the person who has died, in his selection of

Scripture passages or other readings. The prayer will be his most intimate concern. If there is no singing, he may well read a hymn or poem at the close of the service. His one purpose in conducting the service will be to abolish death for the space of half an hour, to banish the shades and shadows of this mortal life, and to lift all present into the sense of the life that is eternal. There will be an intimacy, a personalness, a depth of feeling in all that he says and does that will permeate the whole atmosphere and come home to each sorrowing heart.

This involves the supreme giving of oneself. It means the expenditure of all of one's spiritual energy. A funeral service should exhaust the minister as nothing else ever does. He will know when he has done that he has given all he has. And this will be true each time he officiates. Every new occasion will make the same supreme demand. Formality will be redeemed by the heart which he puts into it. The order of it may vary according to circumstance, but the underlying mood will be the same. He will approach the scene of death with the sense that he has been commissioned to declare that death has lost its sting and the grave been robbed of its victory through him who has brought life and immortality to light. And he will have his reward in the gratitude of those who have turned to him in the hour of their great need. Thus is he a true "minister of God in the priest's office."

Many ministers have grave misgivings about receiving fees for these sacred services. Baptismal fees are rare. Funeral fees are more frequent, yet how can one accept payment for such a service? If it is handed to the minister by the funeral director; or if it comes from a stranger or from one outside of his parish, it can be returned with a courteously worded statement that no honorarium is desired. If it is sent by someone whom the minister knows well, a member of his church, it may be gratefully acknowledged, with the words: "Will you not let me use your kind gift to help someone who will be made happy by it?" Only in exceptional cases, when the terms of the gift make it impossible to decline, will the minister keep it for himself.

What has been said applies also to wedding fees. These are so commonly offered in the expectation that they will be received, that not to do so might seem to be counsel of perfection. Yet, aside from convention, there is no clear reason why a distinction should be made in their favor. Even after weddings does a minister feel wholly comfortable in putting into his pocket a pecuniary reward for having celebrated the sacrament of marriage? If a minister can deny himself this undoubtedly welcome addition to his income, he can add a touch of beauty to the romance of the wedding. He can slip the honorarium inside the wedding certificate which he presents to the bride and say: "You will find a wedding gift from me with this. Please buy something with it for your new home to remember me by." There will be a flush of pleased surprise to reward him and a note may come later telling him what use was made of the unexpected gift. If it be conceded that this is the ideal thing to do, should it not be for the minister the real thing to do? For, in services so intimate, the memory of which is so deep and lasting, should he not aim at perfection?

Ministers Unto Me in the Priests' Office

Thus will one seek to be a true minister in the priests' office. A young woman writing to her minister to thank him for a baptismal service on Easter Day used these words: "I don't believe many ministers think enough — or care enough — for the members of their churches to try to become a personal link between those individuals and Christ. For that is what you have done for me, and I shall never forget it." And what greater thing could any minister do?

CHAPTER 16

The Keys of the Kingdom

✠　　✠　　✠　　✠　　✠　　✠　　✠

PETER had just made his confession "Thou art the
Christ, the Son of the living God." Jesus had told him
that upon this confession, the Church would rest as upon
a rock. Then Jesus added these words: "I will give unto
thee the keys of the kingdom of heaven." Since Peter had
in his heart this innermost experience of God in Christ —
warm, real, passionate, enduring — he had also in his
possession the keys that could unlock doors and admit
into the kingdom of heaven those who were unable to find
their way into it. When we contemplate this symbol we
can hardly resist the feeling that each key opens some
door unto the kingdom of love, of joy, of freedom, of
power. And Peter has them all. He can unlock any of the
many doors into the kingdom. It must be a key — not a
formula, nor a cryptic countersign, nor admonition — but
a key specially designed and devised to make a particular
door open before someone who seeks entrance into the
kingdom. And Jesus, speaking to Peter who is the representative of all who minister in Jesus' name, says that he
has in his hands the keys, not one key but many, which
will open all the doors into the kingdom of heaven. Such
is the spiritual meaning of this word of Jesus to Peter.

Thus there is disclosed another sphere of authority and
of influence which belongs to the minister of Jesus Christ.
All about us are people bewildered and confused. Their
lives are dislocated. They are themselves without inward
poise, control, or confidence. There is a vast amount of
suffering, both mental and moral, in the lives of men

today which can be alleviated only through personal ministration. Without doubt this has always existed, although its cause and cure have not been so well understood as they are today. Beyond question also the conditions of modern life have increased the amount and intensity of this suffering. The pace of life in our day has been too much for its peace. Living is far more complex than it was, with added pressure on the powers of resistance and control. The absence of fixed standards of morals, sophistication, experimentalism, have involved people in moral situations which plague and distress them. Repressions and inhibitions have induced morbidities and neuroses. Because of all this, people are flocking by the thousands to professional psychologists and psychiatrists in their desire to find relief and escape from the problems that beset them.

At this point the ministry has before it an unparalleled spiritual opportunity. It is different from anything else that the minister does. In pastoral visitation, he brings cheer, sympathy, practical helpfulness into the lives of those who are in normal health, or ministers to those who are physically sick. In pastoral evangelism he is making the direct personal, religious appeal to those who may be in no other form of need. But in this sphere he is the spiritual physician, diagnosing mental and nervous and moral problems, helping men to recover faith in themselves, mental balance and moral control, aiding them to find their way unto the kingdom of peace and joy once more. And if he is truly equipped for this special and technical task, he will have in his hands the keys that will open the doors unto the kingdom for many a bewildered, discouraged and even despairing life.[1]

Practically unknown a generation ago, no part of a minister's task today is more filled with spiritual possibilities than this. When once he has acquired the ability to unlock doors for people, this becomes one of the most fascinating and useful aspects of his ministry. Its importance is now so generally recognized that ministers are being specially prepared for it by being trained in personality problems, by serving as internes in psychopathic hospitals, by the study of books now available in abundance which describe the psychological bases of nervous disorders and methods for readjusting a divided and disordered personality. The more knowledge that the minister can acquire in this difficult field, the better.[2] Yet a broad sphere of influence and helpfulness remains in dealing with personal problems for ministers who are not psychological experts in the scientific sense of the term. By careful observation, the exercise of a sound judgment, and a growing experience in dealing with all kinds and conditions of men, any parish minister who is alive to his opportunities, who has himself acquired a true spiritual culture and is deeply interested in people, their needs and their difficulties, can become a wise counselor and

[1] The reader is referred to the author's pamphlet *Pastoral Counseling*, published by the Commission on Evangelism, 287 Fourth Ave., N. Y., from which the substance of this chapter is taken.

[2] For a simple and helpful discussion of this subject, no better book is available than *The Art of Counseling* by Rollo May (Cokesbury Press, 1939). The bibliography will furnish an ample list of books for additional reading.

perform an important and useful work which sorely needs
to be done. Indeed it may be said in all fairness that a wise
religious counselor, a parish minister who really understands his business, may often do more for a sufferer than
the purely secular practitioner or psychiatrist. For there
is no substitute, as professional psychologists themselves
admit, for the purifying power of a real religion.

A change in the status of the Protestant minister from
preacher to "curé," in which the clergyman will diagnose
and prescribe for specific ailments of the souls of man,
was described by Dr. Charles R. Zahniser, then head of the
department of social service in Boston University and professor of applied Christianity, in an address before the
conference of theological students in clinical training at
the Worcester Psychopathic Hospital:

"The new ministry to sick souls must be as scientific in its
process as that which we now require in the physician's work
with sick bodies. Diagnosis must be as accurate and prescrip-
tion as specific. The minister of tomorrow must have a skill in
these equal to that of the psychiatrist, to whose work his will
be in many ways similar. But it is not going to be the same.
"The minister is not to be an amateur psychiatrist or social
worker. His is to be a technique of his own. It has to do with
making the unique contribution of religion itself effective in
the adjustment of a distorted or disturbed and unhappy human
soul.
"The minister has much to learn from the physician, much
from the social worker, but he is not to be a copyist of either,
for religion has a distinct contribution to make to souls in
conflict. That contribution is particularly evident in cases
marked by anxieties and fears, by feelings of inferiority and
depression, or by libidinal urges for which no wholesome outlet has been found. In all of these the basis religion furnishes

for an assuring faith in a good God and the worth in his eyes of every human soul, together with the worthy and satisfying goals it offers on which one's energies may be expended, have values for sick souls which nothing else can afford.

"With more than half of the hospital beds in America now occupied by persons suffering from mental and emotional disturbances largely spiritual in origin, and with crime on the increase because so many have not the moral stamina to withstand the strains of our increasingly complex social life, the work of the skilled physician of souls daily increases in importance." [3]

Dr. Zahniser declared that the day is rapidly approaching when preaching will be incidental to the work of the ministry, although it will not entirely disappear. This change, he said, "marks a wholesome revolution in church program, particularly in Protestantism."

To be an efficient pastoral counselor, it is necessary first of all that the minister should have a genuine interest in people for their own sakes. He must be attracted by them, like to be with them. Their differing personalities will have for him a certain fascination. A minister who cares for anything more than he cares for people will never make a good counselor. Moreover, his interest in them is not primarily because of the good he feels that he may do them; rather they appeal to his imagination and arouse his interest just because of what they are. Moving about among them gives him his deepest happiness and satisfaction. It is a purely impersonal and objective attitude that is native and distinctive, never assumed.

In some way or other, too, people must be attracted to him. Thus he must possess the secret of what is called

[3] As reported in the *Boston Herald,* August 1, 1934.

"personality." In part this will consist of a certain refinement of appearance and manner. Again it will mean tact and insight in dealing with others, a kind of spiritual courtesy and sensitiveness which can be felt more easily than it can be described. Again it lies in a responsive, a quick out-going sympathy with another's need which the sufferer is always able to perceive and to which he naturally and instinctively responds. And deepest of all there must be a goodness, a purity, a holiness upon the part of the pastoral counselor which makes itself felt and makes others feel that here is one whom they can absolutely trust. Let a minister be thus qualified to help erring and unhappy souls and they will of their own accord come to him one after another for counsel and direction, and he will have in his hands the keys that will admit them to the kingdom of heaven. Always the minister will recognize that this vast need is there. He will realize that behind an exterior that may seem respectable, self-satisfied, even sophisticated or cynical, there is this inward suffering all the more poignant because it is repressed or concealed. He will immediately perceive and respond to any cry, however inarticulate, for help and guidance.

The parish minister has unrivaled opportunities for personal counseling. He is being thrown in constantly with people of all ages, in every imaginable emergency in life. He spends his time with them and has, or should have, an intimate knowledge of them. He has access to entire families. He has a broad field of observation and, if he makes use of his rich opportunities, he rapidly acquires a valuable sense of knowledge of human conduct.

No one thus has quite the chance which is his for doing, day in and day out, this delicate and important work. Because he moves among people and sees them under varying conditions, he has a distinct advantage over the professional counselor who sees people only in an office.

Not consciously but by an acquired unconscious habit, he finds opportunities for counseling in his most casual contacts with people. In a chance conversation there may be a moment of confidence. A word let fall gives him all the opportunity he needs. "I wonder if you would care to have a talk about that?" He will not press the point. He will exhibit readiness for an interview without appearing to be too eager. Yet he will be surprised at the number of times that this proffered aid is welcomed. Some of his richest experiences and finest and most rewarding results in personal counseling will come in such fashion as that. What is required and all that is required is the sensitive mind, quick observation, the ready eye and ear, the friendly gesture. All kinds of opportunities lie along the daily pathway of the parish minister. This constitutes what is or should be the romance and poetry of his life.

The minister will never do this kind of work independently of the doctor, for it may very well be that extreme cases of mental and moral disturbance have their origin in physical or nervous disorders. Thus if he confronts the case of one who is suffering from irrational fears or phobias, or if it is apparent that the mind is not acting normally, then the wise minister will seek the advice of either a practicing physician or a neurologist. He will watch carefully for any signs which may indicate the presence of either physical or mental disease. And if he detects it or has good reason to feel that it exists, he will go no further unless competent medical examination assures him that the patient is physically sound and mentally normal, in the sense that he is not unbalanced. Personal counseling can never dispense with either the medical or mental physician. A great deal of damage may be done by amateur psychologists who do not carefully limit the sphere of their operations or understand that there are cases which they are not competent to handle.

When the interview takes place, there will be upon the part of the minister an entire naturalness, an attitude of ease, of friendliness, of simplicity and cordiality. There will be no hint of professionalism in voice or manner, no suggestion of aloofness. It will be a meeting of one friend with another, on the same level. The whole interview will be penetrated by this impression of an easy and unembarrassed atmosphere.

It will begin by an invitation by the minister to the other to tell his whole story, to bring out whatever is on his mind. If the other should hesitate to do this, there will be no urging. On the contrary, the counselor will say: "Perhaps you would rather not." "Please do not tell me anything unless you want to." "Maybe you would rather think it over and come some other time." There will never be any effort on his part to pry into another's secrets or to worm out of him what of his own free will he is not ready to divulge. He will be given the opportunity and every encouragement to do so, but that is all. The counselor will never be curious nor have any desire to know what he has no right to know unless the one who comes to him desires that he shall know it. When the other begins to talk, the counselor will let him talk. He must be a good listener. The major part of the interview for him will consist in just listening. "The secret of influence is to present oneself to each individual as sympathetic intelligence. . . . Every patient is eager to discuss his symptoms with the kindly physician who will listen to him free gratis and for nothing." [4] The function of the counselor is to give the other the opportunity of blurting out into someone's ears what has been pent up within him. Confession, it has well been said, is a cathartic. Its great value lies in giving relief through utterance to an overburdened soul.

While the other is talking, the counselor will be closely observing him without seeming to do so and will be gathering useful information from little signs: of super-nervousness, of evasiveness, of his general condition of mind and body, and these will guide him in his approach to the other's problem. If he has reason to feel that the other is concealing anything, has not really gone to the bottom, he will say: "Is that all? Or is there something else? You had better bring it all out. We cannot get anywhere unless you do. We shall simply be wasting each other's time." Often he will discover in this way that something has been concealed. The counselor will be doing superficial and inefficient work unless he has the whole situation before him.

[4] William J. Locke, *The Wonderful Year*, p. 272. Dodd, Mead and Company, publishers.

He will never be shocked. Or, if he is shocked, he will not show it by the slightest sign. He will remain impassive and imperturbable. As a matter of fact, a counselor of any experience at all is shock-proof. He is not surprised to learn anything about anybody, so many and so varied are the vagaries, the morbidities, the aberrations of which human nature is capable. While he is listening, the minister is quietly selecting the key to the problem. The story ended, he will say, "I understand completely. Possibly I may be able to help you. We are going through this together. We shall fight the same battle, and we shall win the same victory. Your problem is my problem." And this is no mere trick or device. It is an actually felt experience. The minister takes on his own soul the sin and suffering of the patient.

Also, the counselor will always have profound faith in the one who comes to him. Faith in himself is what the patient most lacks. What he instinctively most longs for is that someone shall have faith in him. Nothing must shake the confidence of the counselor that he whom he counsels can and will do the thing which often looms before him as an impossibility. If the counselor confronts people with great expectations of what they can be and may become, these expectations for them and of them will be the very starting point of self-recovery.

He will not exhort, and he will not argue. Usually exhortation leaves the other cold. It rarely does much good and it may do harm. And argument never gets anywhere at all. Neither, however, will he seek to lessen the other's sense of moral responsibility. The tendency to exonerate oneself from blame or to find excuses for oneself will be checked at once by the wise counselor. Often one will blame heredity or environment or circumstance or ineradicable habit for one's failures. The counselor will never lend a sympathetic ear to such pleas. These may have an importance which will be conceded. But not one of them, it should be insisted, is determinative or decisive. It is the business of the counselor to point out that in the last analysis one must accept the responsibility himself for his conduct and for the outcome of his life. As a matter of fact, those who urge these extenuating circumstances themselves often hope that the counselor will not let them off too easily, and respect and are ready to follow an uncompromising summons to heroic action. This brings out the best that is in them, and releases latent powers of performance. The finest kind of sympathy is often an uncompromising form of severity. True sympathy is never soft or enervating; always it makes the other stronger by insisting that the individual has the freedom and capacity to work out his salvation.

Only experience, of course, can enable the minister to make just decisions and to select the right key to the kingdom. Yet as time goes on, he will do so more and more unerringly. He will put this in the hands of the other, who will understand that only his own courage and initiative will enable him to use it. His problem can never be solved for him. It must be solved by him. When the interview is over, he will be given the impulse to action by the counselor's own strong and spiritually invigorating nature. The patient will not be asked to report or to come again. "If you care to see me again, remember that I am always at your disposal" will be as far as the wise minister will go. Because a person has given his confidence once, it does not follow that the counselor is entitled to it again.

These confessions will be held by the minister in strictest confidence. It becomes second nature to him never under any circumstances to mention them. "It is inbred in him not to betray what he has heard by word or sign or in any other way, either in private conversation or in sermon, no matter in what form or under what pretext it is done." [5] The canon law in the Roman Catholic Church says: "The priest who dares break the seal of confession remains under excommunication. The law admits of no exception." This law is equally binding on every minister of Jesus Christ. Yet some Protestant ministers who would not think of speaking of what they have heard in private conversation cannot resist the temptation to use these confidences as illustrative material in sermons. This is a practice to be deplored. It is as truly a betrayal of the confessional as if he told what he knew to a friend of his. It must be sealed up within him as something sacred and inviolate.

The pastor-counselor has in religion a powerful means for the cure of souls, the therapeutic value of which is admitted by modern medical science. The solution of the moral problem lies fundamentally in relating the whole personality to a "God-center." Perhaps one of the greatest

[5] See article "Betraying the Confessional," by Frances J. Nickels, *Christian Century*, January 13, 1937.

arguments for religion is that the religious interest alone is commanding enough, authoritative enough to bring unity and so sanity into a man's life. Put any other principle on the throne and its authority will be challenged by some other competing desire. But when we put God on the throne he can maintain his sovereignty and rule over all the clashing interests and competing desires of a man's life. Thus the minister will seek to bring the other to a recognition of this truth and help him to relate himself to God as the author and preserver of his life.

Again, the counselor will seek to show those who are baffled, bewildered, helpless, feeling that they have come to the limit of their resources and are incapable of escaping from the difficulties in which they are enmeshed, that there is available for their use an immense and inexhaustible supply of spiritual power in the person of Jesus Christ. To come in contact with him is to receive into one's own personality currents of this more-than-human power which will enable them to throw off the burdens that weigh them down and rise superior to temptation or circumstance.

Finally, religion points the way to a manner of life which leads to happiness. For the kind of life enjoined by Jesus was the forgetfulness of self and the discovery of the joy that comes in association with, and the service of, others. "Whosoever will save his life shall lose it, but whosoever will lose his life for my sake, the same shall save it." In this paradox lies the solution of the moral problem of many a life. It is, in a word, the resolute turning from the self-regarding life to a life of objective interest and service. This plain and wholesome precept of Jesus, exemplified in his life, will be offered by the minister to many neurotic souls as the way of escape from their self-pity, from the morass of their own self-regarding lives, into a life of freedom and happiness.

The Christian counselor is never content with the application of purely psychological techniques in dealing with men. Therein lies the important differentiation between him and the secular psychiatrist. He will do well to acquire all the knowledge of these methods that he can. But he has this great advantage: that he holds out to the sufferer the immense help, the glowing hope, the all-sufficient power implicit in the Christian faith. And he presents to him also the warmth, the love, the penetrating sympathy of his own personality in which this faith is a plainly operating reality.

The cure of souls is the greatest of all callings and it needs to be exercised with all the gifts that nature can bestow, with all the knowledge of mental and moral problems that training can give, and with the authority of one who has had put in his hands by divine commission the keys of the kingdom of heaven. To open its doors to many a baffled and bewildered spirit becomes increasingly to the parish minister an absorbing and romantic task.

CHAPTER 17

The Saints Shall Judge the World

✠   ✠   ✠   ✠   ✠   ✠   ✠

E VERY true minister is often overtaken with a certain sense of the futility of his work. He is oppressed with the feeling of his impotence. He cannot see how in any direct way he is exercising any controlling influence on the moral life of the world, which seems to be developing according to certain inexorable and inflexible laws of its own. He is a spectator as events unfold before his eyes, but nothing that he does appears to have the slightest effect in changing the course of affairs or of directing it into new channels. He is going through the motions, he is beating the air, but precisely what if anything is he accomplishing?

He preaches temperance and abstinence, and liquor sales continue to mount. He insists on the evils of gambling, and millions of dollars are expended annually at legalized racing tracks. He talks of peace and the world makes war. He speaks of brotherhood, cooperation and justice between nations, and these shape their policies on the basis of selfish expediency. He pleads for a more just social and economic order, and poverty, destitution, and the inequitable distribution of wealth persist. He is not heeded, and the world goes its way precisely as if he did not exist. Every prophet of God suffers and must continue to suffer from this sense of discouragement and even of despair.

In such a mood, one will do well to go right back to the Gospels and study afresh the method of Jesus. Surely the **world was in** even worse condition then than it is today.

Society was more corrupt. Moral standards were lower. Racial antagonisms were even deeper. War and human slavery had no voice lifted up against them. The world was full of disruptive forces and was held together only by the iron clamp of Rome's power. How now did Jesus order his ministry in such a world and at such a time? What was his attitude, his method? No life ever lived on this planet ever exercised so great an influence or had such power of control as his. If as ministers of Jesus Christ we can imitate him, then our lives cannot be failures; and whatever the outward and visible results of it may seem to be, they must exert in some measure the same kind of influence and possess the same power of control.

We note, then, in the first place a certain detachment in Jesus' attitude toward contemporary events and the secular problems and policies of his day. He lived on a higher level and his mind was not over-occupied and concerned with the details and externals of outward circumstances. Rather, he lived a deep, personal, interior life that found its source and center in the life of God. Thus there appears a certain serenity and sense of security in his outlook upon the world. He was not harried or overborne by the problems presented by the conditions that confronted him because he lived in the constant realization of the strength and peace of God. The channels of communication between his own soul and the life of God were always kept clear and open so that his own life was being constantly reinforced by fresh supplies of divine grace and strength.

We do not need to be reminded of the prominent and consistent place which the practice and cultivation of the presence of God occupied in the life of Jesus. Because of this, his life was clothed with a certain spirituality which both delivered him from anxiety concerning the ultimate outcome of human affairs and at the same time lent him the authority which belongs only to those who are filled with the spirit of God. How helpless the human life of Jesus appears to be before the great imponderable evils of his day. How little did his life and ministry appear to alter or overthrow them. Yet in the light of history we know that there were resident within his soul the moral forces that were destined to topple from their pedestals one hoary evil after another and to set in motion an irresistible power that re-created and is still re-creating the moral life of the world.

We will do well, therefore, as disciples of Jesus, to imitate his attitude toward the external and contemporary and secular life of the world. We will not allow our minds to be too much occupied or enmeshed in the vexing questions of the day. We will keep ourselves informed concerning these, but we will not become so preoccupied with present-day problems which perplex, disturb, and harass the mind, that we shall cease to live on a higher plane, cease to be God-filled, God-inspired men. For only to the degree that we are this do we acquire real significance and become active moral factors in the life of the world and possess any powers of influence and control. Only the cultivation of the life of God, only the possession of the spirit of God will equip us with the peace, the poise, the serenity, the power that will enable us to be in any degree to our world what Jesus was to his.

Thus we will take up our Bibles and seek to know God afresh in the plenitude of his power. We will read the glowing prophecies of Isaiah and of Daniel which so fortified the soul of Jesus. We will read the eighth chapter of Romans and the fourth and fifth chapters of Revelation until the magnificent hope enshrined within them becomes a living part of us, as well as the faith which comes so easily and so naturally out of the discovery of the divine life that we find in them. We must, in a word, become men of spiritual insight and live above the turmoil of the secular world. We must be spiritually-minded men. To move this world to better things, to lift it to nobler purposes, to be amongst those who are the helpers and healers of mankind, it is necessary to have this vantage-ground outside ourselves, outside the world, and that vantage-ground is God.

Always men like that have been powerful factors in the moral life of the world. "Do ye not know," wrote Paul, "that the saints shall judge the world?"[1] Moffatt translates: "Do you not know that you saints are to manage the world?" That surely is a romantic and staggering statement. Yet it has been vindicated in history. Who managed the world in the Apostle's day? Not the emperors or the generals or even the secular philosophers. Rather Paul himself, with the glory of Christ in his heart and the unknown members of those little Christian communities who had in them the spirit of Jesus. These remade the

[1] *I Corinthians 6:2*

233

world in which they lived, however little they could see it or know it.

It will be the same with us if we too have the life of God manifested in Christ at the center of our being. We shall be creating the soul-atmosphere which coming generations will breathe, in which a new world shall be born. For not a single element of any man's life is lost or forgotten. It goes with all its mixture of quality to be inextricably interwoven into the texture of the world's life and thought. Ours, too, shall be creative personalities that will help to shape the destinies of mankind.

In the next place, when we study the method of Jesus, we discover that he spent the short years of his ministry seeking to help individual men and women with whom he came in contact. "He went about doing good." In such humble fashion, with nothing spectacular or sensational about it, did Jesus spend his days. "How much of Christ's life," Henry Drummond has written, "was spent in doing kind things, in merely doing kind things. Run it over with that in view and we find that he spent a great portion of his time in doing good turns to people as he passed by." When we read "that sweet story of old," we find but one Gethsemane and but one Calvary; but we find as many little acts of kindness and of helpfulness as there are stars in the sky.

Jesus did not deal with generalities. He was not concerned with programs and policies. He did not spend his time in furthering movements or plans for the regeneration of the world. Rather he was concerned with the regeneration of the individual man or woman who crossed his path. He seemed to feel that if he saved one individual soul, he was illustrating the method by which alone the world was to be saved. So he let the impact of his personality fall upon the microcosm, the miniature universe which is the soul of man, rather than upon the impersonal universe itself. For in the soul of the individual he found illustrated all the forces of good or of evil that make up the life of the world. If he could cure the soul of one man, he would be showing the method by which the ills that vex the heart of humanity alone can be cured.

We will then seek in our ministry to imitate this method of Jesus. Instead of attempting to find a cure-all for the evils of the world, let us go about as Jesus did, trying to lift individual men and women out of the despairs in which they find themselves. We will resolve to be less and less preoccupied with plans and panaceas and spend more and more of our time as Jesus did, in seeking to solve the problems of the individual man. This patient, careful ministry to the needs of those who look to us for help and healing will be the core of our work, as it was the center of the ministry of Jesus. For the great drama of the outside world has its reflection and reproduction in the heart of the individual man. Tomorrow may be the crisis-hour in his experience; tomorrow may be the zero-hour in his struggle; victory or defeat may depend on such reenforcement as we can bring. If we can help him to win his victory, to that degree are we helping to win the eternal victory of right over wrong, truth over falsehood, good over evil. If we can change the outlook, alter the attitude, meet the need of one individual life, we are doing a work, performing a ministry of lasting meaning and significance. For it is not only a life saved, but, as in the ministry of Jesus, it is an illustration of the way in which alone the life of the world shall be saved.

A young woman once went to the pastor of a certain church and inquired what a Roman Catholic must do in order to become a member of the Protestant Church. He explained to her that this would involve no breaking of the organic bond which already united her to Christ's Church. Her baptism and confirmation were valid. All that was needed was the reaffirmation of her faith and the expression of her allegiance to Protestant principles of worship and order. Afterwards she told him her story. She had been brought up strictly in the Roman Catholic Church to which all of her family belonged. She later married a Protestant and felt that the time had come for her to ally herself with the Protestant Church. When the minister asked how her mother felt about this, he was told that she had disowned her daughter and had broken off all relations with her. The minister asked what she intended to do about that. She replied that there was nothing she could do. Her mother would not even answer her letters. She was reminded that there is a verse in the New Testament which says "Love never faileth" and she was advised to write her mother a love letter every week. Each letter, she was told, would fall like a warm drop of rain on an ice-cake which must ultimately melt.

Sometime afterward the minister went to see her in the city to which she had removed. She told him that the summer previous she and her husband and little boy had driven back to the old home in West Virginia. "Did your mother open the door, run down the path, throw her arms around you and kiss you?" he asked. "That is just what she did," was the answer, "and now I know that love never fails." The minister felt and felt rightly that had he done nothing else for a year, that would have been enough. To have expelled hatred and bitterness from one human heart, to have reconciled two lives that belonged to each other — that was a work of eternal and romantic significance. For in it was illustrated the method and the only method by which human estrangement, whether between individuals or nations, can be healed and men be brought together in brotherhood and peace.

Again, we discover that Jesus spoke to people about God and life and sin and redemption. But he spoke simply and directly. He offered them food, the Bread of Life, that satisfied the hunger of men's souls. He did not talk about the problems of the secular world. There is little in what he said about economics or politics. Neither did he theorize or philosophize or rationalize like the scribes and professors and the dialecticians. He did not argue. He announced. He told them good news in terms that they could understand. He used homely illustrations, called parables, drawn from nature and from life. And the common people heard him gladly. The sheep never turned away hungry. Men marveled at the gracious words that proceeded out of his mouth.

They were indeed wonderful words of life. They have re-echoed ever since in the souls of men. For Jesus spoke of God and the things of God in a way that was fashioned to the deepest needs of men. His preaching and teaching had within it eternal values that touched and still touch the springs of action in men's souls and thus have released spiritual forces which continue to operate in the world. It was effective for its time and for all time. It did not apply to the contemporary problems of the hour and thus become out-moded as these altered from day to day. It dealt with fundamental issues and thus had its lasting influence in shaping the moral life of the world.

Only as we imitate the preaching method of Jesus will our preaching in any wise continue to echo on, and because it, too, touches springs of action in men's souls, become a bit of that spiritual influence that is directing the destinies of mankind. All other preaching ends when the sermon ends. It stops when the preacher stops. It may have entertained, it may have informed, it may have given good advice, it may have contained much that was sound and true. But it was of the moment and for the moment. It had no hint of the eternal in it. It did not speak of the things of God. It awakened no dormant spiritual impulse in the human soul. It did not send men away feeling that they must be, can be, different men from what they were. Hence such preaching is without permanent influence or importance. Such preachers fail to quicken men and so fail to exercise any power or control in the world in which they live. On the other hand, the preacher before the smallest congregation in a village church, if he speaks in faintest accent as Jesus spoke, may have the assurance that what he says, since it finds its lodgment in some human heart and there takes root, has an invisible but lasting influence on the moral life not only of an individual but of the society of which that individual is a part. Such is the romance of real preaching.

Thus we will not often speak of temporary and secular issues. Neither will we rationalize or use academic language. Always there will be an intellectual framework, but this will not protrude any more than the ribs do in one's body. Neither will our preaching be oratorical or rhetorical. The sermons of Jesus were nothing of the sort. And if our sermons are modeled on his, they will seek to be not a work of art, but a piece of bread. We will try to test every sermon by the simple rule: whom will it feed?

There are too few preachers today who preach simply enough. How refreshing it is when one hears one speak whose every accent betrays the cultured and disciplined mind, who is direct and simple in presenting truths which plumb to the depths of human experience. This is the most difficult kind of preaching, for it involves both a knowledge of God and also of the human heart. Yet if we learn from Jesus to preach like that, we may feel that what we say does not end with the saying of it but "makes undying music in the world."

We note also in Jesus' attitude toward the world in which he lived an unslumbering moral indignation against the evils that degraded the souls of men. At times this mounted to white heat as he excoriated the ecclesiastics of his day who were punctilious in their observances of the forms and traditions of religion, yet failed to lift a finger to remove the burden that rests on men's shoulders or rebuked those who caused little children to err or to fall. We cannot overlook the anger of Jesus nor fail to remember that what roused it was not the evil that was done to him but the evils which ruined the souls of men whom he had come to save.

Many of those evils still remain. And, confronting them, we must be capable of the moral wrath and indignation of Jesus. The thing to avoid is complacency, acquiescence, or, if not that, the ability to live in comfort without being stirred and made unhappy by the destitution and misery of others caused by inhuman conditions and practices. It must never be said of us that we have lost the capacity of moral indignation. Moral passion: what is it? It is not the quarrelsome spirit. It is not the querulous or fault-finding temper. Rather it is the staking of the whole man against the wrongs which degrade God's children. For every sinner as bold as Satan there should be a saint as audacious as the Son of God. We must be capable of judging society and secular policies from the high vantage-ground of divine ideas and ideals. We will not pose as amateur authorities in economics or sociology. We will not debate the comparative merits of capitalism and socialism. We will not scold. Rather we will announce the broad principles of Jesus: the dignity of the individual, the sanctity of human life, the motive of service as distinguished from that of selfish acquisition, the conception of the brotherhood of man and the equality of all men before God. And whatever contravenes these principles we will condemn, let the chips fall where they may. If such was the method of Jesus, it will be our method. How uncompromising Jesus was, how little did he accommodate divine truth to human prejudice! We will seek to imitate the moral fearlessness of the Son of Man.

All human progress depends upon the presence in the world of an awakened social conscience. When that conscience dies, the world dies. The supreme contribution of Jesus to the life of the world was to place within it a hatred of evil and beneath it a suffering love that bore that evil away. To share that hatred and that love is to be ourselves, however humble our station, among the saviors of the world.

Thus, in imitation, and only in imitation of the life, the attitude, the method of Jesus, may we have the confidence that our lives, our ministry, our preaching, our influence, have real powers of control in the affairs of men. Perhaps there is nothing in the world so romantic as the undeniable fact that a saintly life manages the world; that its destinies are in the keeping of those who most closely seek to imitate the life of him who, though he lived and labored in humility, has most surely shaped the destinies of mankind.

CHAPTER 18

The Rod of an Almond Tree

✛   ✛   ✛   ✛   ✛   ✛   ✛

J EREMIAH, then a young man living at Anatoth some
four or five miles from Jerusalem, was wandering in
the fields. He had gone out to be alone with his own soul,
to think out the problem of life and duty; and the more
he thought, the more depressed and bewildered he became.
He had been called to a task from which he shrank: to
bear God's message of warning and of judgment to his
own people whom he passionately loved. He felt his own
utter inadequacy for such a mission. He saw the moral
corruption of the nation, the incapacity and irreligion of
its rulers.[1]

Yet the word of the Lord had come to him to oppose
the spirit of frivolity and blindness that everywhere pre-
vailed and to call the people back to the paths of righteousness, to obedience to the word and will of God wherein
alone lay their salvation. And he felt himself unsuited to
that difficult and dreadful duty. He brooded over it and
muttered to himself as he walked along. "Ah, God," he
said, "I cannot speak. I am young and inexperienced.
How can I pit myself against these evils, make men hear
me, bring anything to pass?"

The whole countryside in which he found himself
seemed in strange harmony with his own sad thoughts.
It lay in the grip of winter, bleak, barren, bare. Nowhere
around him was any sign of life. Everything, everywhere
was desolate and dead, just like the nation itself, all winter, no sign of life. But suddenly he stopped. There came

[1] *Jeremiah 1:4–12.*

244

a new look in his face and a new light sprang into his eyes. In the midst of his despairing thoughts about the future of his people, about his own future as the appointed spokesman of God, about his helplessness to alter in any way the currents of the world's life, he had lifted his eyes and caught the sight of an almond tree, bursting into bud and bloom. It was a sudden and startling reminder that, in the midst of that wintry landscape, God was alive. Only a single "rod," just one branch of blossom on a sheltered, sunny bank. Yet all the fresh glory of the spring, all the beauty of summer, all the golden wealth of a coming harvest was prophesied in it. He knew that within a few weeks at most from the bursting of those precocious blossoms, spring would come, surging through a million buds, and all of that bleak landscape would be ablaze with beauty where all had seemed desolate and dead.

The promise of the spring in the bleak of winter, where all had seemed to be death, God awake and at work, turning the wilderness into a garden — that was the message of the almond tree in the heart of Jeremiah. And in the strength of that assurance, he went forth to obey God's call and made his deathless attempt to perform, relying on God's invisible but omnipotent power, what had seemed to him to be an impossible and hopeless task.

And he never forgot that day. Writing years later, a mature man, bearing heavy burdens in church and state, always he remembered that sprig of almond blossom in the midst of a wintry waste that had made God real to him, that had spoken to him of the constant working energies of God; that had saved him from despair, that had put him on his feet; that had told him no matter how hard and barren the soil may be, always God is working on it and within it and under it and bringing fruitful things out of it.

"No," says God. It is not all winter. In the midst of death and desolation, the almond is beginning to blossom. In the fields that seem dead and forgotten, living forces are at work. "Ambushed in winter's heart, the rose of June lies there unfurled." Things may be bad, bad to the point of heartbreak, but it is never all bad. Always there is the rod of the almond tree, the energy of new life, the promise and prophecy of better things to come.

The minister in our modern world repeats in his own experience that solitary walk of the prophet Jeremiah. He, too, has received an authentic summons to be a spokesman for God; he, too, is commissioned to call men to righteousness, to oppose the evil forces in the world, to point men to the richness and inspiration of life which belongs to the Christian faith and to it alone. Yet the prospect looks bleak as he surveys it and he is oppressed with a sense of helplessness.

Alien forces make his spiritual task appear so very difficult. There is the undeniable drift away from institutional religion. People may be loyal to Christian principles and yet remain unconvinced of the necessity of a corresponding loyalty to the Church which incorporates them. And as yet there is no visible turning of the popular tide to the sanctuary. "The Church," it has been said with dogmatic finality, "is now practically impossible as a solution to our present difficulties. [One cannot] honestly contemplate the possibility of a renaissance of faith general enough to make the Church intellectually important again."[2] Intellectualism of one kind or another has replaced for multitudes the deeper intuitions of faith which appear to them to be harmless or unmeaning abstractions unverifiable and ethically inadequate to deal "realistically" with the problems which confront the world. The warfare between religion and science is not over. It has passed its earlier, more superficial phases, but antagonism deep and vital still persists between the scientific and religious approaches to reality. In the sphere of morals, the teaching of the modernists has made its deep impression. The old sanctions have gone and with them the sense of personal responsibility and accountability.

Without the vision of God every man does what seems right in his own eyes. Indeed the very concepts of right and wrong have either lost their meaning or have become strangely inverted so that what was once believed to be right is now held to be wrong, and what once was wrong is now believed to be right. And in the world at large terrible forces have been let loose. It is seething with unrest. Whether we look at political institutions, economic systems, or racial relations, the world is in a state of terrifying instability. No wonder if the prophet in our modern world, cherishing in his heart the precious and glowing truth of the Christian evangel which he is commissioned to utter, is burdened and oppressed.

What now is going to put him on his feet? What will fill

[2] Edmund Wilson: "T. S. Eliot, For Lancelot Andrewes," *The New Republic*, April 24, 1929.

him with courage and quicken his faith? Surely it is the message of the rod of the almond tree. If this could put heart into Jeremiah, it can do the same blessed work for every true prophet of God. God is at work in the resurrection of the springtime, in the lives of all his children, in the reformation of society, in the salvation of the world. Deep down beneath all sight, all knowing, there are the spiritual forces which shall re-create mankind and turn winter into spring. "All winter," said the British soldiers, when at the conclusion of the first world war they surveyed the black and charred battlefields of Flanders and of France. "No," said the spirit of the living God. And when those same soldiers went out ten years later to revisit the same battlefields, they were unable to recognize them. For they were all covered with grass and trees and flowers and sunshine where there had been only death and desolation. "The poetry of earth," as Keats has said, "is never dead."

Here lies the deepest romance of the Christian ministry. He who labors with God and for God can depend in the face of every contradiction, of apparently insuperable obstacles, on this re-creating power and grace. What seems dead is instinct with life. His omnipotent power is always and everywhere at work. To link our lives with God's life is to labor with magnificent assurance, with undying optimism.

All great lives have been lived, all great ministries have been wrought in the faith of the vision of the rod of the almond tree. "All winter," said the philosophers of Greece and of Rome concerning the slaves and the submerged

The Rod of an Almond Tree

classes of that ancient world. "No," said Paul, "I see the rod of the almond tree." In the face of hoary evils which had sunk their roots deep into the soil of a society which seemed impervious to spiritual appeal, he carried to men the energizing gospel of Christ and created saints in Rome and even in Caesar's household. He had the glowing conviction that he who labors "in the Lord" does not labor in vain; that the message of the gospel has within it the seeds of a glorious immortality.

"All winter" was the secular judgment of society in the days before the Reformation, when the spiritual forces of the Church were spent and there was no idealism visible anywhere to re-create the life of man. "No," said Luther and Huss and Zwingli; and a rebirth of religion opened a new chapter in the moral history of mankind. "All winter and dead" might have been said of England in the seventeenth and eighteenth centuries. "Not so," said John Bunyan and John Wesley, "we see the rod of the almond tree." "All winter," said Charles Darwin when he visited an aboriginal race in South America. "No," said the missionary. And on a subsequent visit Darwin himself saw enough of the natives restored to a new life to make him a life-long subscriber to a missionary society. "All winter," said even the churches a century ago of the sunken masses in darkest England. "No," said General Booth, "I see herded in slums and alleys souls that yet shall walk in white robes in the city of God."

In this romantic faith and hope the parish minister will face his task today. Years ago a young Scottish minister who had transferred from his quiet country parish to a

249

city church in Glasgow was standing in a sad frame of mind on the bridge spanning the Clyde, looking at the dark and grimy outlines of the city. Thomas Chalmers, who was passing, stopped, flung his arm around the shoulders of the young man, and pointing to the city said: "Grand field of operations, that." He saw the rod of the almond tree. And we can see it, too. The outlook may not be promising. It may seem as if there were no life. There may be no immediate response to the spiritual appeal. The Christian ethic may appear to be inapplicable to the pressing problems of our modern world. Yet always we may be sure that the energies of God are at work alike in the heart of the individual and in the heart of society. The visible forces will one day disclose themselves. Winter today is sure to be springtime to-morrow.

A great and glowing characteristic of the Bible is that it contains, as Dean Church once said, one unbroken note of hope. Always there is held up before men the vision of a distant, it may be, but sure victory. The Bible leads us through many a dark valley, many defeats and apparently fatal failures. But it ends in a Halleluia chorus and celebrates the joys of the redeemed. For the Bible tells us of a God who is in the thick of the struggle, who pits his strength against the forces which threaten us with destruction. The Cross is the symbol of the final victory of love. It is planted in the center of a scene of cruelty, hate, brutality, and its outstretched arms reach in all directions. It is a grand thing in this reeling world, with everything toppling all around us to be able to say in absolute assurance that the truth as it is in Jesus will prevail inviolate; that nothing can thwart the word and will of God; that his truth, though crushed to earth, will rise again.

The world may look like a graveyard. But in all the calamities of the race there lies concealed the power of a racial resurrection. God is the heir of all things and his throne is never empty. Only as we see the rod of the almond tree, the sign in the midst of all that seems bleak and bare of God's invisible forces working to bring beauty and goodness to life once more, will the prophet of God be given the undying hope that will inspire his life and ministry to its very end. All the equipments of secular disciplines and knowledge, all of our intellectual apparatus are inadequate for our task. There must be something more, something beyond. There must be this perception of a living God whom to know by faith is to be filled with the dauntless enthusiasm that believes all things, hopes all things, endures all things in the sure knowledge that this is the victory which overcometh the world, even our faith.

Thus there is no romance in the world comparable to that of the Christian ministry. In part, as we have seen, that romance is to be found in the dealing with human lives, which present to the minister untold spiritual opportunities which appeal to his interest, his imagination, his sympathetic understanding. His quiet work of parish ministration deepens and broadens every year. He finds himself content even in the smallest parish, with every ambition satisfied. To see the signs of inner progress;

to watch over the growing lives; to meet the sorrows of many people; to be persuaded of the reality of the influence he can wield; to find himself drawn by the deep ties of spiritual affection; to have his days filled with duties that are perpetually fresh with all their sameness; to have the right of entrance to many homes and to many hearts; to be known by all whom he meets; to be able to speak freely on the deepest things in life; to find himself always confronted by tasks which are too great to be measured; and all the time to know the blessedness of human love, to have the memory of happy years — what more romantic life on earth can be lived than that? He may have a baptismal service, a wedding, a funeral service on the same day, certainly within the same week. Let one ponder the infinite significance of each one of these, and who touches life at its very center more intimately, more constantly than he? And his whole life is made up of these things. He deals with human nature in its spiritual relationships. What business on earth is so meaningful as that?

The ministry may be the most arduous, the most difficult, the most precarious of the professions, but also it is the most rewarding. It yields deeper and more lasting happiness and satisfaction than any other. "Always in time of stress, I turn to you." So wrote a young woman to her minister. To know that people in time of trouble will want you, need you: can there be anything more beautiful than that?

And beneath all of this, there is the knowledge that his work is not, cannot be in vain. Always he can see even in time of apparent failure the rod of the almond tree. Others may despair; he never. When all looks like winter, he knows that there are infinite forces at work that can and will bring to life all that is best in man and in the world. He has the romantic hope that is not based on a secular appraisal of life, but rather has its source in the energizing powers of God, the travail of whose soul shall not be satisfied until the kingdoms of this world become the kingdoms of our Lord and of his Christ.

So the parish minister goes his way day by day, rejoicing in the very diversity of interests and activities that fill his days, dealing with almost every type of problem known to human experience, and filled with a hope that never grows dim. Looking back upon it all, he says, I would like to live it all over again. For my life has been pure poetry, real romance from first to last. There is no more romantic career than that of a minister of Jesus Christ.